Osip Mandelstam

Twayne's World Authors Series

Russian Literature

Charles A. Moser, Editor

George Washington University

TWAS 799

Osip Mandelstam, c. 1929.
Photograph by M. Nappelbaum courtesy of Ardis Publishers.

Osip Mandelstam

By Jane Gary Harris

University of Pittsburgh

Twayne Publishers
A Division of G. K. Hall & Co. • Boston

Osip Mandelstam
Jane Gary Harris

Copyright 1988 by G.K. Hall & Co.
All rights reserved.
Published by Twayne Publishers
A Division of G.K. Hall & Co.
70 Lincoln Street
Boston, Massachusetts 02111

Copyediting supervised by Barbara Sutton.
Book production by Janet Zietowski.
Book design by Barbara Anderson.

Typeset in 11 pt. Garamond
by Compset, Inc. of Beverly, Massachusetts.

Printed on permanent/durable acid-free paper
and bound in the United States of America.

Library of Congress Cataloging-in-Publication Data

Harris, Jane Gary.
    Osip Mandelstam / by Jane Gary Harris.
        p.   cm.—(Twayne's world authors series.   Russian
    literature)
    Bibliography: p.
    Includes index.
    ISBN 0-8057-8230-3
    1. Mandel'shtam, Osip 1891–1938—Criticism and interpretation.
    I. Title.   II. Series.
    PG3476.M355Z7   1988
891.71'3—dc19   87-33108
                                                                    CIP

In Memoriam
Joseph Gary

Contents

About the Author

Jane Gary Harris is a professor of Russian literature at the University of Pittsburgh where she formerly chaired the Department of Slavic Languages and Literatures. As part of the Soviet-American Cultural Exchange Program, Professor Harris has spent several semesters in the Soviet Union over the past twenty-five years, primarily doing scholarly research. In 1959, she worked for USIA as a guide at the first American Exhibition in Moscow, explaining American life and culture to thousands of Soviet visitors. The excitement of this experience, which included meeting Soviet writers, artists, and intellectuals, convinced Professor Harris to consider specializing in the field of Russian literature. Six years later in 1965, as a graduate student at Moscow University, Professor Harris was invited to attend Mandelstam's "rehabilitation," and as a going-away gift, was given a "samizdat" (underground, self-published) collection of Mandelstam's verse. Thus began her professional interest in Mandelstam's work. Her first book, *Osip Mandelstam: The Complete Critical Prose and Letters* (1979), was highly acclaimed for its critical perspective and won the 1980 National Book Award for translation. Professor Harris is currently working on a book about Russian and Soviet autobiographical narrative.

Preface

> Like a stone heaven-sent to awaken the earth,
> A line of verse fell in disgrace, not knowing its father;
> The inexorable—that alone is the poet's gift.
> How can it be otherwise. No judge is required.
>
> > (no. 357, 20 January 1937)

> Mounds of human heads move into the distance,
> I grow smaller out there—no one notices me any longer,
> But in books dearly loved and in children's games
> I shall arise to say that the sun is shining.
>
> > (no. 341, 1936–37?)

> Flowers are immortal. Heaven is whole.
> And what will be—is but a promise.
>
> > (no. 394, 4 May 1937)

    This book is dedicated to Memory, to all those whose memories we hold dear and to all those who continue to preserve and bear those memories. This book concerns the privileged memory of a poet, Osip Mandelstam, as it stretches back into the "bookcase of early childhood" and forward as a repository of cultural memory toward "the reader in posterity."

    During the less than thirty years he was granted to make use of his gift, Mandelstam sought to reveal the "nature of the Word" in the origins and roots of human culture, to disclose the promise of human freedom in the continuous process of human creativity, and to preserve mankind's history and heritage through his poetics of cultural synchrony and cultural continuity. In Mandelstam's oeuvre, poetry or "the Word" *is* immortality, for it is the purveyor of ethical, aesthetic, and intellectual values to "the reader in posterity." As Mandelstam recognized so presciently, "the people need poetry," even though it demands obligations and sacrifices, for poetry is the "joy of recognition" of the unity or synchronic bonds between all things—life and death, earth and sky, the man made and the heaven sent.

    Although 1928 may be considered the acme of Mandelstam's career in that it witnessed the publication of his collected works, very little else was to appear in print during the poet's lifetime. In fact, after *Journey to Armenia* (1933), nothing of Mandelstam's was to be published in the Soviet Union for three decades. Mandelstam, like the legendary hero King Arshak in *Journey to Armenia,* became an "unperson." In May 1934, the poet's challenge to his contemporaries almost silenced him completely. He was arrested, allegedly for writing an epigram on Stalin. Miraculously, his sentence was commuted to exile in Voronezh, and what turned out to be a three-year reprieve proved one of his most prolific creative periods. In May 1938, however, he was arrested for the second time and sent to his death.

Being an "unperson" even while he was alive meant that over two thirds of Mandelstam's verse—everything written subsequent to his journey to Armenia in 1930—was unavailable to his readers. Indeed, Mandelstam's last five collections, the two *Moscow Notebooks* and the three *Voronezh Notebooks,* preserved through the superhuman efforts of his wife, Nadezhda Yakovlevna, and other admirers, were only published beginning in 1967, and then outside the Soviet Union, in the four-volume *Sobranie sochinenii* (Collected works) edited by Struve and Filipoff. Inside the Soviet Union, the thaw years of the early 1960s witnessed the publication of a few scattered poems in magazines outside the capital along with some of his "newly discovered" prose. And, although during the 1960s a volume of his selected verse was also prepared for the prestigious Soviet Library of Poets series, no one could be found who was capable of writing a "suitable introduction." Thus it was not until 1973 that the slim blue Soviet volume appeared in print, prefaced at last by a crude excuse for an introductory essay, the third attempt. Nevertheless, the publication of the four-volume collected works in the West and the slow but gradual publication of the poet's writings in the Soviet Union have established Mandelstam's reputation as one of the finest poets of the twentieth century. Indeed, the recent publication (1987) of a collection of the poet's essays and reviews, *O. Mandelstam: Slovo i kul'tura* (O. Mandelstam: Word and Culture) edited by Nerler and introduced by Poliakov, is a sign of renewed interest.

The task of writing this book was a joyous one, although the challenge of presenting Mandelstam's work to an audience unfamiliar with the Russian language was enormous. This book is intended for students of the literature of modernism who enjoy the intellectual, emotional, and linguistic stimulation of modernist art, and the challenge of the medium itself as integral to the pleasure of reading. Like his modernist contemporaries outside the Soviet Union—Proust, Joyce, Pound, Eliot, Wallace Stevens, Yeats—Mandelstam is not "easy." Neither, however, should he be dismissed as merely a "poet's poet," for his prose and verse are intimately connected, and he consciously sought to communicate with "posterity."

While this volume is intended primarily as an introduction to Mandelstam's work for those who know little or no Russian, I hope that those who do know Russian, and those who are already devotees of the great twentieth-century master, will also derive some pleasure by reading this book in conjunction with the Russian texts. Readers who know no Russian are advised to seek out several translations for comparison, and to find someone to read them the original so they may "hear" its music. Readers who are somewhat hesitant about their knowledge of Russian are urged to try to read the originals with the help of this book.

I would like to take this opportunity to express my gratitude to all those who shared with me their time, insights, and enthusiasm for this project, including students, colleagues, and especially my Soviet friends past and present. I am also immensely indebted to all those scholars and devotees of Mandelstam whose contributions are acknowledged in the notes and bibliography, both for their fine analyses and for challenging me to reinterpret individual poems, cycles, and indeed, Mandelstam's oeuvre as a whole. Without their work this book would not have been conceivable, although I take full responsibility for the interpretations presented on these pages.

I would also like to thank the various organizations that have supported this project financially at different stages of its development: the American Philosophical Society, the Harriman Institute at Columbia University, IREX, the Kennan Institute, and the University of Pittsburgh FAS Grants Committee.

And last but not least, I am most grateful to my family for bearing up under the inevitable strains of this project, and especially to my daughter Larissa for accompanying me on a pilgrimage to Armenia in Mandelstam's footsteps.

Jane Gary Harris

University of Pittsburgh

Acknowledgments

I would like to thank Ardis Publishers for permission to use the photograph of Osip Mandelstam in Moses Nappelbaum, *Our Age,* as well as for permission to use Donald Rayfield's translation of "Verses on the Unknown Soldier" in *Russian Literature Triquarterly* no. 11 (1975). I am also most grateful to The Antioch Press for permission to publish excerpts from E.M. Kayden's translation of Pushkin's *Feast During the Plague* in *Little Tragedies: four short verse dramas by Alexander Pushkin* (1965) and to Atheneum Publishers for permission to reprint two poems, nos. 227 and 286, in *Osip Mandelstam: Selected Poems* (1974), translated by Clarence Brown and W.S. Merwin. I am also most obliged to Harvard University Press for granting permission to reprint translations by Stephen Broyde from his book *Osip Mandelstam and His Age* (© 1975 by the President and Fellows of Harvard College); to North Point Press and Professor Clarence Brown for permission to use excerpts from his translation of *Noise of Time* which appears in *The Noise of Time: The Prose of Osip Mandelstam* (Copyright © 1986 by Clarence Brown, translator. Published by North Point Press and reprinted by permission); and to Princeton University Press for granting permission to use Robert Tracy's translations of nos. 42, 48 and 67 in *Osip Mandelstam's Stone* (Copyright © 1981 Princeton University Press. Excerpts reprinted with permission of Princeton University Press).

Chronology

1930   April-November, travels to Georgia and Armenia. Return of lyric voice: Armenian cycle. Moves to Moscow in December.

1931–1933   *Moscow Notebooks* verse.

1933   Summer at Koktebel'; friendship with Andrey Bely. Writes *Conversation about Dante*. Autumn, receives apartment in Moscow. *Journey to Armenia* published. Writes "Stalin Epigram" in November.

1934   First arrest 13 May, followed by exile to Cherdyn. Madness and suicide attempt. Allowed to move to Voronezh.

1935   With the help of his wife, Nadezhda and Sergei Rudakov, writes down all his prose and poetry from memory.

1935–1937   *Voronezh Notebooks* verse.

1937   Freed in May; lives primarily in Savelovo and Kalinin.

1938   Second arrest at writers' rest home, Samatikha, on 2 May. Sentenced to five years of hard labor for "counter-Revolutionary activities." Last letter dated October to brother Alexander from Far Eastern transit camp. Official date of death is 27 December, probably at a transit camp near Vladivostok.

Chapter One

Biography

I well remember the remote and desolate years of Russia, the deaf
years . . . and at seven or eight I was fully abreast of the age . . .
(Noise of Time, 1923–25)

The Early Years

Osip Emilievich Mandelstam's recollections of himself as a precocious
seven or eight year old, "fully abreast of the age . . . ," growing up in
St. Petersburg, the elegant pre-Revolutionary capital of the Russian
empire, grace the pages of his lyrical autobiography, *Noise of Time.*[1]
Nowhere, however, amid those reminiscences that provide most of our
knowledge of the poet's childhood, are the simple facts recorded: that
he was born in Warsaw in January 1891, then under Russian rule; that
his family moved to St. Petersburg shortly thereafter; that he had two
brothers, Alexander (Shura)—whom he loved—and Evgeny—whom
he eventually disowned as brother because of his callousness; that he
was apparently an excellent student; and that he undoubtedly had a
rather happy, normal childhood.

In *Noise of Time,* Mandelstam does not acknowledge family or personal relationships as formative influences on his developing consciousness; rather he sees a certain legacy of cultural memories and a keen
sensitivity to speech patterns as his family inheritance: "The speech of
the father and the speech of the mother—does not our language feed
throughout all its long life on the confluence of these two, do they not
compose its character?" (84). Furthermore, he claims that the place in
his reminiscences where a "family ought to have been" was filled with
books and keen observation. His parents are portrayed almost exclusively through references to the language that expressed their person-
alities, to the books they read and loved, and to the special gifts with
which they endowed their impressionable son—a passion for music and
poetry from his mother and a highly individualized sense of philosophical inquiry from his father. Although Emil Veniaminovich Mandel-

1

stam is characterized by a peculiar "languagelessness," it prevented him neither from becoming a successful leather merchant nor from nurturing a passion for philosophy. Born Flora Osipovna Verblovskaya, Mandelstam's mother is depicted as speaking "pure Russian," although "her vocabulary was poor and restricted." She was also a devotee of Pushkin and a fine pianist. As members of St. Petersburg's Jewish intelligentsia, his parents were primarily concerned with their sons' upbringing, that is, providing the best education possible, first by hiring a "series of French and Swiss governesses," later by enrolling them in the best schools.

Mandelstam's childhood memories, as recorded in *Noise of Time,* are filled with colorful images of St. Petersburg as "sacred and festive," as a splendid monument and "elegant mirage":

And I say now, without a moment's hesitation, that at the age of seven or eight all this—the whole massif of Petersburg, the granite and wood-paved quarters, all the gentle heart of the city with its overflow of squares, its shaggy parks, its islands of monuments, the caryatids of the Hermitage, the mysterious Millionaya Street, where there were no passers-by and where only one small grocery story had wormed itself in among the marble, but especially the General Staff Arch, the Senate Square, and all Dutch Petersburg I regarded as something sacred and festive.

. . . It always seemed to me that in Petersburg something very splendid and solemn was absolutely bound to happen. (72–73)

Mandelstam's recollections overflow with lyrical reminiscences of childish "cravings" and "inspirations," of emotional pleasures drawn from the feeling of living in a dreamworld, in a "mirage," and poetic assertions of how his "delirium" transformed his beloved city and his vision of the world, protecting him from the chaos, catastrophe, and change that would so dramatically alter his life in the future:

The Petersburg street awakened in me a craving for spectacle, and the very architecture of the city inspired me with a kind of childish imperialism: I was delirious over the cuirasses of the Royal Horse Guard, the silver trumpets of the Preobrazhensky band. . . .

The elegant mirage of Petersburg was merely a dream, a brilliant covering over the abyss, while round about sprawled the chaos of Judaism . . . showing through the chinks of the stone-clad Petersburg apartment. . . . (74–77)

On the other hand, while these reminiscences compel us to assume that Mandelstam must have had a fairly happy and protected childhood, beneath the superficial splendor of the "deaf years" the sensitive young poet already hears rumblings of agitation and uncertainty, chaos, catastrophe, and change: the "noise of time."

Intellectually and spiritually Mandelstam identified with St. Petersburg, renamed Petrograd, and then Leningrad after the Bolshevik revolution. The significance of his association of St. Petersburg with Russian literary, cultural, and spiritual traditions is matched only by his mythic vision of the city as Petropolis, Persephone's city,[2] and his fear for the destruction of Russian culture. Some of his most poignant lyrics are dedicated to St. Petersburg, while *Noise of Time* is a testament to his love for the city as the intellectual and cultural milieu of his childhood and youth. Later, though he spent many years of his life as an itinerant, as a man without a permanent residence card, and as an exile, St. Petersburg remained "my city." "I returned to my city, familiar to the point of tears, / Familiar as veins, as mumps from childhood years" (no. 221, 1930).[3]

When he was nine Mandelstam's parents succeeded in entering him in the Tenishev Commercial School, one of the finest, most exclusive, and most progressive schools in St. Petersburg. Except that it was a day school, it was based on an English model: "On Zagorodnyi Prospekt, in the courtyard of a huge apartment house . . . about thirty boys dressed in shorts, wool socks, and English blouses played soccer. . . . They all looked as if they had been transported to England or Switzerland and there fitted out in a way that was neither Russian nor that of a Gymnasium student, but somehow rather Cambridge in style. . . . we received our education in . . . high glass boxes with steam-heated windowsills. . . . our huge classrooms [seated] 25 students. And our corridors were not corridors but riding halls with tall ceilings and parqueted floors . . . (90–92).

The intellectual atmosphere was stimulating as evidenced by the boys' interest in both their curriculum and their teachers. It was there that the young Mandelstam encountered not only Marxist doctrine in the form of Kautsky's *Erfurt Program*, but the writings of Avvakum, the remarkable seventeenth-century religious martyr. The curriculum was politically and educationally liberal. It also included a thorough grounding in Latin and a full survey of Russian literature up through early symbolist poetry.

Mandelstam's vivid portrait of his teacher and mentor, Vladimir Vasilievich Gippius (V. V. G.), and his lively portrayal of his school years indicate how positive an influence this institution had on his formative years. It provided an "attitude toward life":

No, Russian boys are not English. You won't catch them with sport or the boiled water of political amateurism. Life, with its unexpected interests and passionate intellectual diversions, life will burst into the most hothouse-like . . . Russian school, as it once burst into Pushkin's lycee.

. . . Everything which represented an attitude toward life was greedily devoured. I repeat: my schoolmates could not endure Belinsky due to the diffuseness of his attitude toward life, but Kautsky was respected, and Protopop Avvakum, whose autobiography, in the Pavlenkov edition, was part of our study of Russian literature.

Of course, none of this could have been without V. V. G., the moulder of souls and teacher for remarkable people. . . . (100)

Wanderings and Searchings

Graduation was followed by a period of profound intellectual and spiritual seeking, poetic apprenticeship and experimentation, travel and study. Young Mandelstam spent 1907–8 in Paris, 1908–9 back in St. Petersburg, and 1909–10 in Heidelberg before officially enrolling in the University of St. Petersburg in the autumn of 1911.[4]

In April 1908 Mandelstam wrote a letter to Gippius, self-consciously reviewing his year in Paris and evaluating his quest for spiritual unity, a religious or philosophical worldview. He tries to explain his search and to elucidate the nature of his attraction-repulsion toward what he terms Gippius's "principle . . . of religious culture," "some dear yet hostile principle, the charm of which lay in its duality." As the only major document extant from this period of Mandelstam's youth, and as the only document expressing his intellectual and spiritual strivings at the age of seventeen, a large portion of this letter is worth citing. It is important to note that at this point Mandelstam's conscious sense of religion, philosophy, and politics was quite vague and nondoctrinal. Rather, his letter expresses his enthusiasm, his joie de vivre—love of "life, faith, and love," and his "passion for the music of life." Occupied almost exclusively with "poetry and music," he is also full of plans for travel, plans for a "systematic study of literature and philosophy," and plans for writing:

Having been raised in a milieu where there was no religion (family and school), I have long been striving hopelessly and platonically, but ever more consciously, toward religion. My first religious experiences go back to the period of my childish passion for Marxist dogma and are inseparable from that passion.

But for me the bond between religion and society was severed when I was still a child. At the age of fifteen I passed through the purging fire of Ibsen, and although I did not hold out on the "religion of will," in the end I stood firmly on the soil of religious individualism and opposed society.

I accepted Tolstoy and Hauptmann, the two greatest apostles of love for the people, ardently yet abstractly, just as I accepted the "philosophy of the norm."

My religious consciousness never rose above Knut Hamsun and his worship of "Pan," that is, of an unacknowledged God, and to this day that remains my "religion" . . .

In Paris I have read Rozanov and love him very much, but I do not like that concrete cultural content to which he is devoted with his pure, Biblical devotion.

I have no definite feelings toward society, God, or man, but for this very reason I love life, faith, and love all the more.

All this should help you understand my passion for the music of life which I found in a few French poets and, among Russian poets, in Bryusov's school. They captivated me by their ingenious boldness of negation, pure negation.

I live quite alone here and am occupied with almost nothing except poetry and music.

Besides Verlaine, I have also written about Rodenbach and Sologub and am planning to write about Hamsun. After that, some prose and poetry. I plan to spend the summer in Italy and, after I return, to enroll in the University and to make a systematic study of literature and philosophy. . . . (*CPL*, 475–76)[5]

Of Mandelstam's earliest verse we know only that he had begun writing while still at the Tenishev School, that he was invited back to give a reading the autumn following his graduation, and that in 1909–10 he sent numerous poems to Vyacheslov Ivanov, leader of the Russian symbolist movement, whose gatherings he attended at Ivanov's "Tower."

His first published poems (nos. 8–9, 13–14, 147)[6] all reflect aspects of symbolism, the dominant literary movement of the first decade of the twentieth century. They appeared in the August 1910 issue of *Apollon*, the new journal founded by Innokenty Annensky, Nikolay

Gumilev, and Sergey Makovsky. *Apollon* not only took over the role of the *Scales* (*Vesy*) upon the demise of that symbolist organ, by publishing the debates of 1910–12 on the so-called "crisis of symbolism," but gradually became the organ of the symbolist heresy, Acmeism. Thus, when Mandelstam returned to St. Petersburg in October 1910, after a year at the University of Heidelberg, he essentially came home to witness the death throes of symbolism and the rise of two new symbolist heresies, futurism on the one hand, Acmeism on the other. In the autumn of 1911, Mandelstam not only enrolled in the University of St. Petersburg, but joined Nikolay Gumilev's Poets' Guild, the nucleus of the future Acmeist movement.

Much of Mandelstam's earliest verse reappeared with only slight variations in his first published collection, *Stone* (*Kamen'*). The appearance of this slight green book, printed at the author's own expense, coincided with the publication of Acmeist manifestoes and programmatic verse in the March 1913 issue of *Apollon*, gaining him instant recognition as one of Russia's finest young talents. Technically elegant and bursting with original perceptions and striking imagery, *Stone* doubled in size upon republication three years later.

With the outbreak of World War I, Mandelstam began working for the "Union of Cities," a St. Petersburg organization providing war relief. Exempt from military service because of poor health, he spent parts of 1915, 1916, and 1918 in the Crimea, where he met and became briefly involved with Marina Tsvetaeva, then a barely recognized young poet. Most significant, perhaps, at this time the Crimean motif enters his verse, alone and in juxtaposition to the imagery of St. Petersburg, now perceived as Persephone's cold and bleak Petropolis.

Civil War and the 1920s

In 1917 Mandelstam was in Petrograd to greet the revolutions, first the February coup when Kerensky's provisional government replaced the Czar, and then the Bolshevik takeover the following October. During this period Mandelstam was employed by the Peoples' Commissariat for Education. By May 1918 he had moved to Moscow, the new Soviet capital, along with the Soviet government.

Although Mandelstam's initial poetic response to the October Revolution (no. 192, "When October's favorite was preparing / A yoke. . . ." ["Kogda oktiabrskii nam gotovil vremenshchik / iarmo

. . ."], printed in the 15 November issue of the Socialist Revolutionary newspaper *Volya Naroda* [People's Freedom]) was quite hostile, particularly in his use of derogatory terms to depict the revolutionaries and in his portrayal of Kerensky as a crucified Christ figure,[7] by 24 May 1918, less than six months later, when no. 103, "The Dawn / Dusk of Freedom" ("Sumerki svobody"), appeared in *Znamya truda* (Banner of Labor), his position was far more complex and ambiguous. Indeed, the poem centers on the semantic ambivalence of its title.[8]

In the midst of the Civil War, which raged from 1918 to 1921, Mandelstam not only visited Kiev, where he met his future wife, née Nadezhda Yakovlevna Khazina, but while courting her witnessed the expulsion of the Soviets and the city's capture by the White Army. Promising to return shortly, Mandelstam left for the Crimea and Georgia, where he was arrested first by the Soviet authorities in Batumi and then by Wrangel's White Guards in the Crimea. Another two years passed before he and Nadezhda were finally reunited. They were officially married in 1922. That same year they moved to Moscow, living first in Herzen House—the Union of Writers' official residence for writers—on Tverskoy Boulevard, and then in an apartment they found by chance on the Yakimanka, in the Zamoskvorechie section of Moscow. In addition, 1922 saw the publication of *Tristia,* Mandelstam's second collection of poetry, containing verse written between 1916 and 1921. And this was also the year of his acquaintance with Nikolay Bukharin, who became his major Party benefactor. In her memoirs, Nadezhda Yakovlevna characterizes Bukharin as just "as impulsive as M":

We had first started "going to see" Bukharin in 1922 when M. had asked him to intercede for his brother, Evgeny, who had just been arrested. M. owed him all the pleasant things in his life. His 1928 volume of poetry would never have come out without the active intervention of Bukharin, who also managed to enlist the support of Kirov. The journey to Armenia, our apartment and ration cards, contracts for future volumes (which were never actually published but were paid for—a very important factor, since M. was not allowed to work anywhere)—all this was arranged by Bukharin. His last favor was to get us transferred from Cherdyn to Voronezh.[9]

The early 1920s proved to be an extremely prolific period for Mandelstam. His intellectual and aesthetic growth was exhibited in expressions of greater self-consciousness, in his awakened interest in literary prose as well as poetry, and in his focus on the personal challenge of living in the new Soviet age. He sought to express his allegiance to the revolution without sacrificing his almost biblical sense of moral consciousness and humanistic values. He sought to absorb into the poetics of cultural continuity predominant in his earlier collections, *Stone,* and *Tristia,* new themes of contemporary consciousness and conscience. It was also during the 1920s that Mandelstam tried his hand at translating in order to earn a living, but found this highly distressing because it left him no time for his creative work. As he wrote in a letter to his father during the winter of 1923–24: "What am I doing? I'm working for money. The crisis is grave. It's much worse than last year. But I've already made some progress. There were more translations, articles, and so forth. . . . World Literature [Publishing House] is loathsome to me. I dream of quitting this nonsense. The last time I worked for myself was in the summer. Last year I still worked for myself quite often. This year—not at all . . ." (*CPL,* no. 19, 489–90).

In 1924 the Mandelstams moved to Leningrad, first to an apartment on the Morskaya in the center of the city, and later to an apartment in the writers' colony at Tsarskoe Selo, just outside Leningrad, where they remained through most of the 1920s. Nadezhda's health demanded that she have fresh air, and during this period she also spent long stretches of time in the south recuperating from tuberculosis. From 1924 on, Mandelstam began to experience ever greater intellectual and creative limitations. His letters of 1924–26 are filled with complaints about his financial difficulties and the "suffocating" work of translation. By 1925 he had ceased writing verse entirely; a period of poetic silence began that continued for five years. Nevertheless, his masterpieces of literary prose date from this period: *Noise of Time* (*Shum vremeni,* 1923–25), *Egyptian Stamp* (*Egipetskaia marka,* 1927), and "Fourth Prose" ("Chetvertaia proza," 1929–30), each of which reflects a turning point in his own creative biography as well as in his prose style. In a letter of February 1926 he proudly wrote to Nadezhda that "*Noise of Time* provoked a 'storm' of ecstasy and enthusiasm in the foreign press, for which we can be congratulated" (*CPL,* no. 25, 495). These were followed by two more unique prose works, *Journey to Armenia* (*Puteshestvie v Armeniiu,* 1931–33) and *Conversation about Dante* (*Razgovor o Dante,* 1933), both of which continued his autobiographical investigations under different generic guises.

The year 1928 marked the highpoint of Mandelstam's career as a published writer. The intervention of his political patron, Bukharin, made possible the publication of a three-volume set of his collected works: *Poems,* including *Stone, Tristia,* and a new cycle, *1921–25*; *Egyptian Stamp,* a collection of prose, including *Noise of Time*; and *On Poetry,* a selection of his critical essays.

On the other hand, Mandelstam's work as a translator was becoming ever more distasteful to him. His essays on translation—"Torrents of Hackwork" ("Potoki Khalturi," April 1929) and "On Translation" ("O perevodakh," July 1929)—are part of his polemic against the literary establishment, which reached its peak with the so-called Eulenspiegel Affair of 1928–29.

Mandelstam had been commissioned by the Land and Factory Publishing House to revise two earlier translations of *Till Eulenspiegel,* by A. G. Gornfeld and V. N. Karyakin, for a new edition published in 1928.[10] However, without the knowledge or consent of either Mandelstam or the original translators, the title page listed Mandelstam alone as translator. Although the frustrated poet claimed in a desperate letter to the newspaper *Evening Moscow* (*Vecherniaia Moskva*), no. 288, 1928),[11] to have informed Gornfeld of the situation immediately, Gornfeld quickly charged him with plagiarism, and the affair assumed the proportions of an ad hominem political scandal. In May 1929 Mandelstam felt obliged to write another letter, this time to the *Literary Gazette* (*Literaturnaia gazeta*), criticizing the wretched state of Soviet translations and translators, while demanding that an attack on him by the notorious hatchet man David Zaslavsky be "called by name" (*CPL,* no. 64b, 328–29; *SS,* 2:480). Zaslavsky "answered" the same month with an attack so crude that it provoked a letter to the *Literary Gazette* in Mandelstam's defense signed by such leading Moscow writers as Boris Pasternak, Mikhail Zoshchenko, Alexander Fadeev, and Valentin Kataev, among others.

The affair was finally resolved, however ambiguously, by the Federation of the Unions of Soviet Writers (FOSP) in a resolution stating that although Mandelstam had been subjected to unfair attacks, he was morally at fault since no proper contract had been drawn up with the original translators. Nevertheless, the repercussions of this affair still resounded even after Mandelstam wrote the unpublishable "Fourth Prose," excoriating the entire literary establishment, and long after Bukharin saw to it that he was sent off on his long-desired journey to Armenia.

The Armenian sojourn to which Mandelstam nostalgically referred as his "200 days in the Sabbath land," seemingly released him once again to write lyric poetry. The return of his lyric voice came in October 1930, at the conclusion of his journey. The resultant Armenian cycle was to be followed by the *Moscow Notebooks* of the early 1930s and the *Voronezh Notebooks* of 1935–37.

The Final Decade

Upon his return to Soviet Russia, Mandelstam found himself still persona non grata in Leningrad. Realizing that he would never again find work or obtain a residence permit there, he reluctantly moved to the Soviet capital. After living for a while with his brother Alexander, with Nadezhda's brother Evgeny, and then again in the Herzen House on Tverskoy Boulevard, the Mandelstams were finally able to move into a small cooperative apartment in the autumn of 1933. The summer of 1933 they had joyfully spent in Old Crimea and then in a Koktebel Writers' Home where Mandelstam developed a close friendship with the prominent writer Andrey Bely.

For all their difficulties, the Moscow years proved enormously fruitful poetically. Indeed, 1933 even witnessed Mandelstam's spectacular acclaim in his beloved city of Leningrad for a reading of his verse at the Hotel d'Europe, an occasion recorded for posterity by the literary critic Boris Eikhenbaum.[12]

One year later, however, on 13 May 1934, Mandelstam was arrested for the first time. His manuscripts were confiscated and he was banished to Cherdyn, a small town in the Ural Mountains, where he apparently suffered an attack of madness marked by an attempt to commit suicide by jumping out of a hospital window. Luckily, he only broke his arm. His sentence was commuted—seemingly thanks to Bukharin's intervention with Stalin—to three years of exile in Voronezh, in the heart of the "black earth" belt of Southern Russia. The Voronezh years were physically and mentally debilitating. Mandelstam's heart condition worsened, and his nervous disorder grew so severe that he was overwhelmed by anxiety and unable to breathe each time Nadezhda had to leave him to go to Moscow to find work or to obtain money. Nevertheless, these years also proved to be extremely prolific. Indeed, his last five collections—the two *Moscow Notebooks* and the three *Voronezh Notebooks*—comprise two thirds of his extant verse. Preserved through the superhuman efforts of his wife and other admirers, they were published posthumously, first in editions outside the

Soviet Union, and now gradually within, thus assuring Mandelstam's reputation as one of the twentieth century's finest Russian poets.

Mandelstam's last year of freedom—beginning with his release on 16 May 1937 and ending with his second arrest and final disappearance on 1 May 1938—was spent wandering from town to town along Moscow's hundred-mile perimeter, since former exiles are not permitted to reside in major Russian cities.[13] The Mandelstams lived primarily in Savelovo and Kalinin, taking occasional trips to Moscow to obtain food and money from friends. Nothing survives from this period.

Mandelstam's second arrest took place at the isolated writers' rest home in Samatikha. He was sentenced to five years of hard labor for "counterrevolutionary activities." Death overtook him, from what evidence we have, in a transit camp near Vladivostok in December 1938. His last letter, from October 1938, addressed to his brother Alexander, contains the return address "Vladivstok, USVITEL, Barracks No. 11" and a desperate plea for money and warm clothes (*CPL,* no. 97, 573–74).

Hope Against Hope, Nadezhda Mandelstam's first book of memoirs, details her husband's last years from his first arrest for composing the so-called "Stalin Epigram" (no. 286) to his second arrest and final disappearance. By accompanying him throughout this period, Nadezhda Yakovlevna quite literally kept him alive. Her account concludes with a careful sifting of the rumors about the poet's last days.[14] *Hope Abandoned* is no ordinary sequel. It is a book of judgment written by an eyewitness. Not only does the survivor-heroine ruthlessly attack the moral deafness and degradation that supported Stalinism, but she celebrates her victory over time and her "faith in the abiding value of poetry and its sacramental nature." In these books she also tells with passion and immediacy, eloquence and integrity, the story of her own incredible survival, and illustrates her devotion to her husband and to the preservation of his work.

From 1934 to 1964, Nadezhda Yakovlevna lived in exile, condemned to the wretched existence of a "politically suspect wife," dedicated to her primary task: the preservation of Mandelstam's oeuvre and his "rehabilitation." After years of wandering, teaching English in various schools, doing translations to eke out a living, and writing when time permitted, she was given a small apartment in Moscow's Cheremushki district in the southwestern sector of the city, which, in the 1970s, became a gathering place for Soviet and foreign visitors and devotees. Nadezhda Yakovlevna lived and wrote her memoirs there until her death on 29 December 1980.

Although the official date provided on Mandelstam's death certificate is 27 December 1938, his second arrest condemned him to the realm of "unpersons" (like his hero, King Arshak, in *Journey to Armenia*). Only in August 1956, three years after the death of Stalin, was the beginning of his official "rehabilitation" even conceivable. The commission appointed in 1957 by the Writers' Union to oversee the poet's remains included the poet's widow, her brother Evgeny Yakovlevich Khazin, the poet Anna Akhmatova, the writer Ilya Erenburg, and the critics Zinovii Paperny, Alexander Surkov, and Nikolay Khardzhiev. Not until 1973, however, did a large selection of Mandelstam's poetry appear in the Soviet Union in one of the familiar blue volumes of the Poet's Library series. And only recently, in 1987, a volume of his essays and reviews has appeared entitled *Word and Culture*. Outside the Soviet Union, the first post-Stalin publication of Mandelstam's work appeared in New York in 1955. His *Collected Works* (*Sobranie sochinenii,* 1964–81) have been continually updated, making the available four-volume edition reasonably complete. Most of Mandelstam's prose and verse may also be found in translation.

Chapter Two
Symbolism, Acmeism, *Stone*

> For the Acmeists the conscious sense of the word,
> the Logos, is just as magnificent a form as music
> is for the Symbolists. ("Morning of Acmeism," 1913)

Symbolism

The Russian symbolist movement,[1] which had dominated Russian literature and culture since the turn of the century, had revived interest
in the art of poetry. *Scales* (*Vesy*), edited by Valery Bryusov and Andrey
Bely from 1904 to 1909, not only transformed the reading habits of
the St. Petersburg elite, but set out to influence taste in art, music,
and philosophy by introducing Western European literary and artistic
movements into Russia, in particular, the ideals and values of French,
Scandinavian, and Flemish symbolism. By about 1906, however, the
year preceding Mandelstam's school graduation, the Russian symbolist
"establishment" underwent a schism. Ivanov, Bely, and Blok, generally
regarded as the "second generation" symbolists, asserted their views
that poetry and art served as exclusive instruments for the attainment
of religious, mystical, and metaphysical experience.

In contrast, those poets regarded as the "older generation"—Annensky, Bryusov, and Sologub, among others—adhered to the more secular
aesthetic credo of French symbolism enunciated by Baudelaire and developed by his followers, Verlaine, Rimbaud and Mallarmè, that poetry
was autonomous and hence an end in itself, and that the poet's task
was to perfect his craft, not just to record visions of otherworldly experiences, mystical encounters, or dreams.[2] The themes of the "older
generation" reflected a more pessimistic, often decadent, vision of life,
looking back to Baudelaire's *Les Fleurs du mal,* specifically to his conception of the duality of life and his view of man as positioned between
two conflicting impulses, between reaching out to something beyond
the present world—to God, spirituality, or the ideal—and the sensation of being continually sucked back into the abyss, into the horrors
of this world—"spleen." While Baudelaire recognized his dilemma as

metaphysical, he attempted to resolve it through aesthetic means by drawing momentary analogies or "correspondences" between the poet and his work of art, or his union with another human being. Baudelaire's poem "Correspondences," in which nature is compared to a "forest of symbols," expressed this fundamental view and was taken by the symbolist movement as a programmatic statement. Thus, aesthetic truth expressed in the act of poetic creation came to be perceived as the only source of unity in the world, and poetry as an autonomous activity. On the metaphysical level, symbolist poets were concerned with the recovery of unity, which they sought through poetic or artistic experience, or in the expression of the search for such experiential moments. On the technical level, they were preoccupied with form as the means of capturing and perfecting those moments, and with the creative process itself—the act of finding, experiencing, and recording "correspondences." As late as 1921, in his essay "Word and Culture" ("Slovo i Kul'tura"), Mandelstam praised Baudelaire and his followers as the "last Christian martyrs," who faced their dilemma directly and thus transformed it into art.

The second generation of Russian symbolists, on the other hand, resolved Baudelaire's dilemma by conceiving of poetry as *the means* to religious experience or mystical transcendence, not merely as an autonomous aesthetic process. Their themes reflect a philosophical idealism and metaphysical optimism inherent in their faith in the possibility of escaping this world.

Inspired by the philosophical teachings and poetry of Vladimir Solovev, and by his "discovery" of the poetry of Fedor Tyutchev, they emerged as far closer to the ideals of German romanticism than French symbolism. Indeed, Solovev and Dmitry Merezhkovsky, the first to celebrate Tyutchev's mystical and metaphysical insights, declared that his verse sought to reveal the chaotic and mystical essence of existence.

Subsequently, Tyutchev's role in Russian poetry has been compared to that of Baudelaire in French poetry, for he is perceived as the first poet to express modern man's metaphysical striving in a world that no longer believed, and his poetry is understood as an effort to discover belief. Georgette Donchin points out that the older symbolists "did everything to credit Tiutchev with the theory of correspondences . . . [while] the second generation truly discovered Tiutchev at the same time as Baudelaire . . . [whose] 'correspondences' was instrumental in the appreciation of Tiutchev as a forerunner of Russian Symbolism."[3]

Basically, both generations of Russian symbolists found in Tyutchev a Russian metaphysical poet, a national figure, who expressed the isolation of the individual, emphasized the mysteries of the universe, and taught aspects of Schellingian idealism—that the universe has a dual nature since it is divided into two worlds, Cosmos (the world of life, order and beauty) and Chaos (the abyss or nothingness). More important, perhaps, the symbolists read Tyutchev to understand Chaos as the ultimate reality, in that it alone animated Cosmos. The second generation symbolists were particularly influenced by Tyutchev's German romantic ideals, by his Schellingian pantheism, nature philosophy, and revelations of sublime spiritual and metaphysical truth, which they sought somehow to combine with Russian orthodoxy. Hence, Tyutchev's influence on Russian symbolism was profound, but his significance was primarily metaphysical, rather than aesthetic owing to the general philosophical interpretation of his work.

Mandelstam's earliest extant verse reflects a profound consciousness of symbolism and its conflicting traditions. He exhibits a formidable aesthetic concern with problems of technique and form and recognizes the metaphysical basis of his subject matter.

Most significant, between 1908 and 1911, Mandelstam seems to have anticipated his role in the history of Russian poetry, foreshadowing his task both in the preservation of the Russian and Western European cultural heritage and in its transformation, suggesting his position as intermediary, as facilitator of a "dialogue" between past and future, between poetic movements, directed toward his "reader in posterity."

In one of his earliest poems Mandelstam enunciated the poet's role as the synthesizer and preserver of two traditions—the serious, moral philosophical poetry of oratory and grandeur represented by Tyutchev and Russian metaphysical symbolism, and the purely aesthetic ideal suggested by the doctrinal statements of Baudelaire and realized in the lighter, more whimsical verse of Baudelaire's followers, especially Verlaine.

As early as 1908, in his poem "In the spontaneity of creative exchange" ("V neprinuzhdennosti tvoriashchego obmena," no. 498), Mandelstam formulated this poetic credo for the first time. He suggested that the creative act is in part an "exchange" or "interchange," that it reflects continuity as well as transformation, and that the poet is a craftsman who "artfully" links past and present in a creative synthesis by imparting his own imprint to the union.

Specifically, Mandelstam contrasts Russian poetry, represented by

"Tyutchev's austerity," with Verlaine's "childlike" whimsy, implying that the symbolist poetry of his day required a dose of Verlainian spontaneity. Indeed, he questions the tradition of "grandeur" in Russian poetry and asks where "its vernal kiss and birdsong" are to be found.

> In the spontaneity of creative exchange,
> Tell me who might artfully combine
> Tyutchev's austerity with Verlaine's whimsy,
> Imparting an imprint of his own on the union?
> Grandeur is so much a part of Russian verse,
> But where are its birdsong and vernal kiss?
>   (no. 498, 1908)

Indeed, Mandelstam's early verse reflects his credo, his superb knowledge of Russian and French poetry, and his efforts to absorb their essential features into his poetic creation.

"Tender Evening, Significant Dusk" ("Vecher nezhnyi, sumrak vazhnyi," no. 457f), sent to Ivanov in 1909–10, is another good example, for it reworks thematic material from several of Tyutchev's poems, "Grey-Blue Shadows Merged" ("Teni sizye smesilis"), "Dream at Sea" ("Son na more"), and "There is Melodiousness in the Sea Waves" ("Pevuchest' est' v morskikh volnakh"). Nevertheless, Mandelstam not only merges Tyutchevian images and develops the earlier poet's ambivalent use of Schelling's philosophical concept of chaos as a positive creative force, but already manages to transform Tyutchev's poetic material for his own purposes.

In "Tender Evening, Significant Dusk," the poet-persona is first overwhelmed as "Blind joy entered" and "filled our hearts"; then as "Dark chaos deafened us" and the "drunken air stupefied us," "lullabies" were chanted by "an enormous choir: Flutes, lutes and timpani. . . ." The irony and whimsy here recall Verlaine's poems in which flutes, mandolins, and even drums appear to soothe the soul or emerge as part of the soul's landscape, for example, "Claire de lune," "Crimen Amoris," or "Bruxelles."[4]

Mandelstam's subjective persona rejoices in Tyutchevian nature and is overwhelmed by mysterious music, but in his poem music is no longer just Tyutchevian music from which the "soul" of man is somehow isolated, separated. Rather, the concluding stanza acts as a kind of Verlainian whimsical realization of the poet-persona's desire: to be overwhelmed by the bright, lively, and loud choir of "flutes, lutes, and timpani," not merely the distant, impersonal music of nature.

In contrast to Tyutchev's "austerity," the waves and even the air itself become intoxicated, tipsy. Instead of serious philosophical questions posing the anticipated Tyutchevian conflict between man and nature, Mandelstam's poem concludes with a rising cadence and three dots, suggesting that the subjective persona is literally overwhelmed by "lullabies." Furthermore, instead of a Tyutchevian "merger," we find an ironic "mixup": everything's tipsy, intoxicated, stupefied, joyful, and overwhelmed by music—music inspired equally by "evening tenderness" and "dark chaos." Instead of appealing to oblivion or annihilation to escape this world, the poet rejoices in the elements of this world, first in the "wind," then in the waves and chaos that inspire him to create. Thus, a kind of Verlainian emotional indulgence combined with whimsy and irony reverse the anticipated Tyutchevian "austerity" and pessimism.[5]

By the time of his first publication in August 1910, Mandelstam was already moving beyond the Tyutchev-Verlaine antithesis to define his own unique imprint. For instance, in such poems as no. 8, "Given by body . . ." ("Dano mne telo . . .," 1909), which was reprinted in 1913 in *Stone,* Mandelstam's poet-speaker puzzles over the very gift of being—his own physiology—and contemplates how to "use" his body, how to transform his "breath," into something immortal. Mandelstam thus meditates on the poetic process itself, on the work of poetic transformation. Again, in his earliest extant essay, "François Villon," dating from 1910, concern with the physical, with the "here and now," with the "things" of experience, becomes more evident. He begins to develop themes that foreshadow the later essays and verse of the symbolist heretic, the emerging Acmeist poet.

By the following year, in no. 21, "A cold meager ray . . ." ("Skudnyi luch kholodnyi . . ."), the poet-speaker finds the symbolist firmament not a goal but a burden: "the firmament is silent, is dead"; it has nothing to say, for "the heights are orphaned and mute." On the other hand, he finds "a cold, meager ray" that "sows light in the damp wood," and he recognizes inner feelings which must be sung:

> . . . Slowly I carry sorrow
> Like a grey bird in my heart.

> What shall I do with this wounded bird?
> (no. 21, 1911)

In the final stanza, morning breaks, and though the poet is but "half awake", he recognizes in its tenderness a "vague chiming of thoughts. . ."

In the autumn of 1911, Mandelstam officially left the symbolist fold to join Nikolay Gumilev's Poets' Guild, the nucleus of the future Acmeist movement.

Acmeism

Acmeism, like any literary movement, is difficult to date. The year of its formal establishment as a closed circle of poet-friends sharing a consciously prescribed poetics, as a movement with a name, manifestoes, and a journal, is 1913. The six self-declared Acmeists whose verse "illustrations" appeared in the March 1913 issue of *Apollon* included Nikolay Gumilev and Sergey Gorodetsky as the movement's founders and theoreticians, Anna Akhmatova (Gumilev's wife) and Osip Mandelstam as its most celebrated poets, and Vladimir Narbut and Mikhail Zenkevich as its loyal adherents.

Although 1913 has been viewed as the culmination of Acmeism, efforts were made after World War I to redefine its significance. As late as 1961, Akhmatova, in her autobiographical sketch, "Something about Myself," loyally referred to herself as "an Acmeist." In her memoirs, she cites Mandelstam's 1928 letter commemorating Gumilev's shocking and untimely death on 25 August 1921: "My conversation with Kolya [Gumilev] has never been interrupted and never will be."[6] Nadezhda Mandelstam in her memoirs praises Zenkevich's steadfast reverence for his Acmeist past, and reminds readers of her husband's definition of Acmeism: "not only 'nostalgia for world culture,' but also an affirmation of life on earth and social concern."[7] Thus, far from being a short-lived literary movement, Acmeism was to transcend time by assuming the function of "moral and aesthetic memory."

The history of Acmeism may be traced back to the conscious reassessment of symbolism by its heirs and critics and to the self-conscious expression of the as yet unnamed new tastes, directions, and values initiated on the pages of Apollon in 1909–10 with the publication of Innokenty Annensky's critique of symbolism, "On Contemporary Lyricism" ("O sovremennom lirizme"). By the end of 1910 an aesthetic opposition to "second generation" symbolism was taking shape as Gumilev and his adherents began to formulate their new poetics. By 1911, abstract philosophical issues were replaced by more pragmatic tasks: thus the key words in Gumilev's "Letters on Russian Poetry" ("Pis'ma o russkoi poezii"),[8] appearing monthly in *Apollon,* were "talent," "taste," and "poetic craft." *Apollon* became the de facto organ of the "third generation" modernist poets.

Highly significant for establishing the tenets of Acmeism was Gumilev's reference to Oscar Wilde's evaluation of "the word" as the universal aesthetic medium: "The material used by musicians and artists is poor by comparison to the word." A few years later in his essay, "Morning of Acmeism," Mandelstam advocated raising "the word" to the position of honor held by "music" in the symbolist canon.

Furthermore, as early as 1910 in his essay "François Villon," Mandelstam began to conceive of the function of poetry as the actualization of the human experience in all its precision, vitality, and complexity. The means to this end, he indicated, lay in the poet's capacity to wield precise details as opposed to the "suggestive" language of symbolism. Poetic craft should allow the reader to relive the poet's experiences vicariously, making the "passing moment. . . . endure the pressure of centuries." Mandelstam thus added a sense of historicity to Gumilev's emphasis on the "word"—the idea that revelation of the historical experience is also a poetic challenge.

Indeed, the publication of "François Villon" in the March 1913 issue of *Apollon,* accompanied by Gumilev's translation of fragments from Villon's *Grand Testament* and the careful selection of poems illustrating the Acmeist manifestoes published the preceding January, may be regarded as Mandelstam's first printed manifesto. Somewhat later, in "Morning of Acmeism" ("Utro Akmeizma") written in 1913, but published only in 1919 in Narbut's Voronezh magazine *Sirena*, he reiterated in more elegant and complex language most of the aesthetic principles first elaborated in 1910: balance, precision, dynamism, complexity, and physiological power as expressed through "the word."

The term "Acmeism" was first coined by Gumilev in his "Letter on Russian Poetry" of September 1912, a review of Sergey Gorodetsky's *Willow (Iva)*. Along with synthesizing elements noted earlier—the concept of the aesthetic universality of "the word," the "feeling for the eternal in the momentary," irony as a fundamental poetic element, and the poet-craftsman's ideal as "the precise embodiment of emotional experience"—he underscored Acmeist "mythopoesis": "*Acmeism is in essence mythopoeism,* because what, if not myth, will the poet create who repudiates both the exaggeration peculiar to youth and the uninspired moderation of old age . . ., who accepts the word in all its dimensions—musical, pictorial and ideological, and who demands that every creation be a microcosm. Criticism has frequently noted the domination of the subject over the predicate in Symbolist poems. Acmeism found this predicate in the logically musical and continuously developing movement of the image-idea throughout the entire poem."[9]

The manifestoes published in January 1913 included Gumilev's "Acmeism and the Precepts of Symbolism" and Gorodetsky's "Some Currents in Contemporary Russian Poetry." While Gorodetsky's manifesto was primarily an antisymbolist polemic, Gumilev's was a historically oriented, pragmatically focused assessment of the symbolist legacy and a relatively precise definition of Acmeism's "new directions." Gumilev cited as his literary models Shakespeare, Rabelais, Villon, and Theophile Gautier, for they best expressed man and his inner world, man and his physical delights and powers, man's capacity for life, and man's need to express his experience in artistic form: "To unite these four elements is the Acmeists' dream," he wrote.

In addition, Gumilev emphasized the need to recognize "the unknowable," for there is beauty in the "naive but wise and painfully sweet sensation of one's own lack of knowledge: this is what the unknown gives us." On the other hand, he stated that while Acmeists respect the unknown, they distinguish between "the artist's material," which may include "angels, demons . . . spirits . . . as poetic images," and thought systems, dogmas, and doctrines, that require justification outside the realm of poetry. Hence, Acmeists do not seek resolutions in social, philosophical, or religious doctrine, because what matters is "being," "the existence of the phenomenon."

It was Mandelstam, however, in both his manifesto "Morning of Acmeism" and his later essay "On the Nature of the Word" ("O prirode slova") who suggested that the essential distinction between symbolism and acmeism lay in its semantic or philological consciousness, for the ultimate "reality" *is* "the word": "Too often we fail to see that the poet raises a phenomenon to its tenth power, and the modest exterior of a work of art often deceives us with regard to the monstrously condensed reality contained within. In poetry this reality is the word as such." He points out the nature of the confusion:

"The word as such" was born very slowly. Gradually, all the elements of the word were drawn into the concept of form. To this day the conscious sense, the Logos, is still taken . . . for the content. . . . The Logos demands nothing more than to be considered on an equal footing with the other elements of the word. The Futurists, unable to cope with the conscious sense as creative material, frivolously threw it overboard, repeating the crude mistake of their predecessors.

For the Acmeists the conscious sense of the word, the Logos, is just as magnificent a form as music is for the Symbolists. (*CPL,* 61–62)

Like the symbolists, the Acmeists valued technique and craft. However, while their favorite techniques included irony, poetic distance, and a sensitive use of visual and psychological imagery—often psycho-physiological imagery—their predecessors showed a general preference for ideological (theoretical, philosophical, and religious) vision, immersion in "the moment of transcendence," and often a superimposed or artificial use of musical and religious imagery.

Also in keeping with the symbolists, the Acmeists retained the idea of the "word" as an autonomous entity, the sacred "Logos." Mandelstam in particular emphasized the semantic value of words, the basic "verbal fabric" of poetry, as distinct from symbolist "suggestiveness." The Acmeists did not forgo thematic content for technique, as Mandelstam accused the futurists of doing, and never advocated "throwing Pushkin overboard," but on the contrary created a cult of Pushkin.

Among the poems illustrating the manifestoes were Gumilev's "Iambic Pentameters" ("Piatistopnye iamby"), Gorodetsky's "Adam," Narbut's "She is Not Beautiful" ("Ona—nekrasiva"), Akhmatova's "I Came to relieve You, Sister" ("Ia prishla tebia smenit', sestra") and "Cabaret Artistique," Zenkevich's "Elk's Death" ("Smert' losia"), and Mandelstam's "Hagia Sophia" and "Notre Dame," both republished in *Stone.*

"Iambic Pentameters" contains Gumilev's autobiographical reckoning with his youth as well as inspired, self-confident prophecy. His persona ironically derides his "dazzling dreams" as he details the nature of his romantic failure. He affirms instead a newly discovered joy in working with a community of poet-masterbuilders to create monuments "pleasing both the heavens and the earth." The sharp, relatively spare imagery of the love lyric is juxtaposed to physical and metaphysical imagery uniting the poet's emotional commitment to poetry, Acmeism and Freemasonry.

Both in his verse and in "Morning of Acmeism," Mandelstam echoes Gumilev's image of the poet as self-confident, joyous builder. He focuses primarily on the poet-speaker's experience of intellectual and mystical awe before the very fact of "existence" and suggests an architectural analogue that likens "the word" as the poet's "material" to the "keystone" of the Acmeist edifice. His spiritual reckoning and awe are responses to his cultural legacy, aroused by such monuments as Notre Dame and Hagia Sophia. In "Morning of Acmeism" he states: "To exist is the artist's greatest pride. He desires no other paradise than existence. . . . Love the existence of the thing more than the thing itself and your own existence more than yourself: that is Acmeism's highest commandment . . ." (*CPL,* 61).

Mandelstam associates the poet-architect's "material" with the "existence of the thing," and the artist's "reality" with "the word." To celebrate his physical and metaphysical joy in "existence," the Acmeist builds monuments from "the word" whose "monstrously condensed reality" expresses the "noble mingling of rationalism and mysticism and the perception of the world as a living equilibrium."

Mandelstam's programmatic poem, no. 39, "Notre Dame," combines the doctrines of "Adamism" and "Acmeism" with the credo of "Morning of Acmeism." As an "Adamist," he draws an analogy between the sheer physicality and might of the great stone cathedral of Notre Dame and Adam's powerful physique, creating an image of the cathedral as a dynamic, living organism. The cathedral is also revealed as if joyously perceived anew by Adam—not only the first man on earth but the first human artist and poet, the giver of names. As an "Acmeist," he underscores the significance of both the historicity and continuity of art's highest forms, the "acme" of human creativity, at the moment of creation and as continuous inspiration for posterity. Beauty is awesome to Mandelstam in both its external and internal forms as well as in its physiological and metaphysical manifestations of the unexpected and unfathomable. Meaning is simultaneously rational and mystical, historical and eternal, momentary and recurrent. Through the mediation of his art, the poet synthesizes what might appear to be antithetical values, perceptions, and images, thus converting complexity and mystery into forms comprehensible to man's common cultural experience.

It is within this context that Mandelstam presents the poet's function as a kind of apprentice-craftsman to the monuments of the ages. In structuring his own poetic monuments, he unites the material of his craft with his cultural legacy, juxtaposing the concrete act of external observation of the material phenomena and their organization to his emotional, aesthetic, and metaphysical experience. By studying the inner logic of the aesthetic "organism" of Notre Dame, he perceives it anew, transforming it into yet another, more dynamic monument appropriate to his own age. Thus, monuments of the past are revealed simultaneously as dynamic impulses, as vehicles of awe and surprise, and as concrete reminders of cultural continuity.[10]

Stone

The publication of *Stone* (*Kamen'*, 1913), Mandelstam's first volume of poetry, coincided with the publication of the Acmeist manifestoes and programmatic verse in *Apollon*, gaining him instant recognition as one of Russia's major new talents. In 1916, *Stone* was reissued in an expanded version containing eighty-one poems, thus doubling its original size.

Many of Mandelstam's early poems, in particular those published in *Stone*, were concerned with the precise depiction of human culture and the actualization of the human experience. Their themes ranged from the human body itself (no. 8, "Given My Body, What Use Shall I Make of It," 1909) to the choreography of a tennis match ("Tennis," 1913) or even a parody of the silent film (no. 50, "Silent Movie," 1913); from a comparison of silence and muteness (no. 14, "Silentium," 1910) to eloquent praise of Bach and Beethoven (no. 46, "Bach," 1913; no. 72, "Ode to Beethoven," 1914); from unique depictions of splendid spiritual monuments (no. 38, "Hagia Sophia"; no. 39, "Notre Dame," 1912) to poignant tributes to Russia's cultural capital, St. Petersburg (no. 42, "Petersburg Stanzas"; no. 48, "The Admiralty," 1913), to the ancient cultural capital of Europe, Rome (nos. 56, 61, 65–66, 69, 79–80, 1913–15) and to Europe at large (no. 68, "Europe," 1914; no. 70, "1914," 1916).

For example, the opening stanza of "Notre Dame" sets up an analogy between the cathedral's inner, organic structure and man's physiological essence: the cathedral, compared to Adam, is perceived as "tautening its nerves" and "flexing its muscles." In the second stanza, the poet-persona views the exterior form of the cathedral, grasping "its secret plan" with the observant eye of the Acmeist poet-craftsman: he contemplates the technical details making the complex structure a reality. Stanza 3 focuses on the complexity of art and reiterates the doctrine expounded in "Morning of Acmeism," which links Mandelstam's worldview to the ideal of the Middle Ages: "the noble mingling of rationality and mysticism and the perception of the world as a living equilibrium." The poem concludes with the speaker's confident asser-

tion of the poet's self: the pronoun "I," absent from the earlier stanzas,
is reiterated three times.

> Where a Roman judge once judged an alien race—
> A basilica now stands, both joyous and first,
> Like Adam once, tautening its nerves,
> The light cross-vaulting flexes its muscles.
>
> From the outside the secret plan gives itself away:
> Here powerful flying buttresses forestall
> The cumbersome mass from shattering the wall,
> And restrain the bold vault's battering ram.
>
> Elemental labyrinth, unfathomable forest,
> The rational abyss of the Gothic soul,
> Egyptian power and Christian meekness,
> Reed next to oak; everywhere the plumbline is king.
>
> The more attentively, O fortress Notre Dame,
> I studied your monstrous ribs,
> The more I thought: from dead weight
> Someday, I too shall create a thing of beauty.

(no. 39, 1912)

Mandelstam thus presents the Acmeist poet's function as recognizing "the existence" of earthly phenomena and revealing their physical
and metaphysical beauty to his fellow man, so they in turn may celebrate their "existence." Ten years later in his essay "On the Nature of
the Word" Mandelstam invokes Bergsonian intuitionism as well as
moral and social consciousness as dimensions of Acmeism, focusing his
discussion on "the word" as "verbal representation." In 1913, however,
he centers his attention on the aesthetic autonomy and complexity of
"the monstrously condensed reality" and on the continuity of art, opposing both the symbolist emphasis on otherworldliness and the fu-
turist disdain for tradition and cultural heritage.

"The Admiralty" is another fine example of Mandelstam's Acmeist
principles, applied in this instance to his beloved St. Petersburg, emphasizing its place in the cosmos. This vital, complex but precise depiction of Peter the Great's Admiralty, with its spire topped by a ship
weathervane, standing majestically over the Neva embankment, looking out toward the open sea, again celebrates both a man-made mon-

ument and the dynamic aesthetic and spiritual power behind it. It is another tribute to human creativity and vision.

> A dusty poplar droops in the northern metropolis,
> The translucent clockface is lost among the leaves,
> And through the dark green a frigate or acropolis
> Gleams in the distance, brother to sky and sea.
>
> An airborne ship and unreachable mast,
> Serving Peter's heirs as a yardstick,
> Teaches that beauty is no demi-god's whim,
> But a simple carpenter's cunning eye.
>
> While four sovereign elements benignly rule us,
> Man in his freedom has created a fifth.
> Does not this ark, so austerely constructed,
> Deny to space its supreme command?
>
> Capricious medusas clinging in anger,
> While anchors rust like abandoned plows—
> But see our three dimensional bonds are severed,
> And all the seas of the world open before us.
> (no. 48, 1913)

In addition, Mandelstam's first volume contains numerous reminiscences of literary models past and present—Homer, Racine, and Ossian, Edgar Poe and Dickens, Pushkin, Annensky, Blok, Akhmatova, and Tsevetaeva. Literary references and subtexts[11] have varied functions in Mandelstam's verse. One may be the basis of a polemic, another might serve as a major source of inspiration. A poem might also be part of a dialogue with a favorite poet-friend, living or dead. Above all, Mandelstam strives to convey, both in his verse and in statements of his poetic credo, his theory of the synchronic nature of cultural history, that the "blessed legacy" of world culture binds him to the artists and monuments of all time. Two fine examples to follow:

Petersburg Stanzas (for N. Gumilev)

Above the yellow of government buildings
The swirling snow fell thick through the day;
Pulling his overcoat close, a law student swings
His arm out wide, and settles back in his sleigh.

Steamers are moored until spring. Where the sun
Is hot the thick glass of cabin windows glows.
Russia, like some enormous dreadnaught,
Lies at her dock in ponderous repose.

The Neva has embassies from half the globe,
The sun, the Admiralty, and silence.
And the state is wearing a stiff purple robe
As poor as a hair shirt worn for penitence.

The heavy weight a northern snob must bear—
The ancient burden of Onegin's anguish;
The wave of a snowdrift on the Senate Square,
Smoke from a fire, a bayonet's cold flash. . . .

Skiffs scoop up the water, and the gulls
Swoop down to gather on the rigging warehouse
Where *muzhiks* wander, selling drinks and rolls,
As if they were an operetta chorus.

A line of cars rushes through the haze;
Ashamed of his poverty, his walk sedate,
Queer proud Evgeny, with his absurd ways,
Breathes gasoline and curses his fate!
                    (no. 42, 1913; trans. R. Tracy)[12]

I had never heard Ossian's stories[13]

I had never heard Ossian's stories,
Had never tasted that ancient wine—
Why does a glade appear before my eyes
Where the blood moon of Scotland shines?

I seem to hear, against a brooding silence,
Harp music mingled with a raven's croaks
And underneath the moon I catch a glimpse
Of clansmen slipping past in wind-tossed cloaks.

I have received a blessed legacy—
A foreign poet left me his wandering dreams;
And we can freely choose to think scornfully
How dull our kindred and surroundings seem.

> And this may not be the only precious thing
> That skips over grandsons, passing to their sons,
> And a skald reshapes once more another's song
> And sings it as his own.
>
> (no. 67, 1914; trans. R. Tracy)

Furthermore, during this period between the first and second editions of *Stone*, Mandelstam wrote several essays that testify to his intellectual, spiritual, and poetic values. While "François Villon" may be considered his first printed Acmeist manifesto, and "Morning of Acmeism" and "On the Addressee" ("O Sobesednike") successive statements of his Acmeist credo, "Pushkin and Scriabin" (begun in 1915, but completed only in the early 1920s) reassesses the poet's "consciousness of being right" as a fundamental characteristic of his interpretation of the "Christian artist," defined in that essay as a free spirit, absolutely unburdened by "necessity." In direct contrast, the essays on Chaadaev and Chenier (also dating from 1914–15) indicate the young poet's profound concern with intellectual and moral issues, his abiding interest in the question of freedom and necessity, and his serious involvement with the problem of the artist and society. By providing an extraordinary insight into his self-image, these essays foreshadow Mandelstam's metaphor of the "*raznochinets*-writer" (the writer as critical intellectual and social outcast, whose allegiance is to the "fourth estate"), created as his autobiographical hero and self-portrait in *Noise of Time* (1923–25), reiterated in the 1930s, and applied to Dante, Pushkin and himself in *Conversation about Dante* (1933).

"Peter Chaadaev" is particularly significant, for it links the image of the "*raznochinets*-writer" with Russia itself, and cites "moral freedom" as the essence of Russian cultural identity, establishing its vital function in every subsequent Russian writer's worldview. According to Mandelstam, the fact that Chaadaev dared to admit that Russia was cut off from the West and therefore had nothing to offer history but its own essence, allowed him to contemplate Russia in a new, positive light, as a "free" entity—free from the West's legacy of petrified forms and ideas, free to realize the necessity of choosing its own moral and spiritual path. Chaadaev's journey to the West and his independent decision to return home to Russia are viewed as an unprecedented act of moral commitment. Chaadaev becomes a metaphor for Russia's cultural legacy: "moral freedom."

Equally significant, Mandelstam was intrigued by the stimulus

Chaadaev's writings provided for the definition of his own views on poetic freedom and morality. After "Peter Chaadaev," this issue is pursued once again, although from opposite points of view, in "Pushkin and Scriabin" and "Remarks on Chenier," emerging many years later in "Fourth Prose" and *Journey to Armenia*.[14]

"Pushkin and Scriabin," although extant only in fragments, is Mandelstam's most extreme defense of the doctrine of "art for art's sake." It introduces the reader to his unique definition of "Christian aesthetics," a concept created out of efforts to characterize Christian art as not much more than artistic freedom clothed in Christian terminology and based on a purely aesthetic reading of the Redemption as "divine illusion." According to Mandelstam, by offering mankind divine grace, Christ relieved him of all "necessity," permitting him henceforth to live the free, joyous, and unrestrained life of the innocent child. Only the Christian artist is capable of celebrating this state of "joy," for he alone is "free" to experience it. Mandelstam rejoices here in the idea that Christian art is free of the "tragic pathos" of pre-Christian art: "It is 'art for art's sake'. . . . No necessity of any kind . . . darkens its bright inner freedom, for its prototype, that which it imitates, is the very redemption of the world by Christ. Thus, neither sacrifice nor redemption in art, but rather the free and joyous imitation of Christ is the keystone of Christian esthetics . . . (*CPL,* 91).

Pushkin, in the guise of a completely free and independent spirit, the defender of "art for art's sake," is Mandelstam's model in this essay, just the obverse of the "austere" Tyutchev in the verse of 1908. By 1915 Pushkin has replaced Mandelstam's earlier models of the poets of "birdsong and the vernal kiss," of the childlike whimsy and delight, unfettered by the burdens of "necessity."

While this romantic extremism did not hold Mandelstam long, as a moment in his intellectual biography, it represents a significant development of the Tyutchev-Verlaine antithesis broached in his earliest verse and continued in the Acmeist essays.

"Remarks on Chenier" ("Zametki o Shen'e"), on the other hand, evolves as a kind of intellectual counterpoint to "Pushkin and Scriabin." While Pushkin appears as an independent spirit and defender of "art for art sake" in contrast to Scriabin, in "Remarks on Chenier" morality (echoing "Peter Chaadaev") is recognized as an essential element of Pushkin's aesthetic vision expressed through his admiration for Andre Chenier, poet of the French Revolution. Chenier, we know, did not distinguish between the writer as a free individual aware of his capacity as an artist and the writer as a social being responsive to society, but envisioned the artist as an active social force. Courage to protest was considered a sign of a great writer.

Similar ideas recur in Mandelstam's essays and literary prose, from *Noise of Time* to "Fourth Prose." The poet's right to challenge temporal values in the name of "the word" emerges as a major theme in his work of the 1920s and 1930s.

Another significant aspect of Mandelstam's appraisal of Chenier is his discovery that "Chenier ingeniously found the middle road between the classical and romantic manner." In his struggle to identify his own path, Mandelstam finally recognized in the early 1920s that his ideological and aesthetic impulses were primarily classical or neoclassical, thus they obliged the poet to devote equal attention to technique and text. In contrast to the romantic and later symbolist traditions in which the poet views himself primarily as a seer or visionary, often emphasizing the dichotomy between the intuitive and interpretive mind, the classical vision served as an inspiration to what Mandelstam would call "the mind seeking unities and connections," by demanding that the poet perceive himself as the interpreter of truth and take cognizance of his reader.

Thus, by 1922, in "On the Nature of the Word," Mandelstam prepared to broaden his definition of Acmeism to encompass elements from both the classical and romantic traditions. "The wind of Acmeism turned the pages of the Classicists and the Romantics, opening them to the page which most appealed to the age. Racine was opened to *Phedre,* Hoffmann to *The Serapion Brothers.* Chenier's *lambes* were discovered along with Homer's *Iliad"* (*CPL,* 131).

What is more, in his redefinition of Acmeism, Mandelstam found a compromise that satisfied his sense of civic and moral obligation. He pointed out that the poet's duty to the state is not the highest form of moral commitment; his highest duty is to confront time itself in the name of the "word." Consequently, the poet's obligation is not merely to support the state by educating its "citizens"; his obligation is to teach his fellow "Men": "Acmeism is a social as well as a literary phenomenon in Russian history. With Acmeism a moral force was reborn in Russian poetry. . . . Until now the social inspiration of Russian poetry has reached no further than the idea of 'citizen,' but there is a loftier principle than 'citizen,' there is the concept of 'Man' . . . As opposed to the civic poetry of the past, modern Russian poetry must educate not merely citizens, but 'Men'" (*CPL,* 131).

Mandelstam's poetry and prose henceforth followed new directions, suggested partly by the essays on Chaadaev and Chenier, but expressed only in his subsequent collection of verse, *Tristia,* in his essays of the 1920s, and in *Noise of Time.*

Chapter Three
Tristia

Only one care have I left in this world:
The golden need to ease the burden of time.
(No. 108, "Sisters, heaviness and tenderness," 1920)

The telling title of *Tristia* defines Mandelstam's second book of verse, written between 1916 and 1921. In contrast to the celebratory mood of *Stone,* this collection illustrates how an ambivalent, often negative, lyric impulse serves the poet's more mature poetic voice. In *Tristia,* he begins to confront the demands of history and change on poetry and culture, examining the premise that art can "ease the burden of time."

Poetic maturation is evident in Mandelstam's philosophically and psychologically complex mythopoesis as well as in his semantically dense poetics of association. Keenly aware of the enormous social and political upheaval wrought by the Revolution, and gravely concerned over its effect on cultural continuity, he sought to assimilate discontinuity and change into his mythopoetic system. He clarifies this idea in "Badger Hole" (Barsuch'ia nora"), his tribute of 1922 to Alexander Blok: "Poetic culture arises from the attempt to avert catastrophe, to make it dependent on the central sun of the system as a whole, be it love, of which Dante spoke, or music, at which Blok ultimately arrived" (*CPL,* 137).

The Uses of Ambiguity

Mandelstam's effort to assimilate the "burden of time" into his poetics renders unique his most politically acute poem on the Revolution, "The Dawn/Dusk of Freedom" (no. 103, "Sumerki svobody," 1917), where his philosophical and psychological ambivalence toward historical change is reinforced by the device of ambiguity characterizing the poem's structure.

Semantic ambiguity is immediately evident in the poem's title, which cannot be translated unambiguously, and in the first stanza.

31

Although the title and opening imperative seem to place this work among the typical political hymns of the day, Mandelstam actually transforms the contemporary idiom through a very complex reading of the historical context:[1]

> Let us glorify, brothers, the dawn/dusk of freedom—
> The great crepuscular year.
> Into the seething night waters
> The massive forest of nets is lowered.
> You will rise in deaf, god-forsaken years,
> O sun, judge, people.
>
> Let us glorify the fateful burden
> Which the people's leader assumes in tears.
> Let us glorify the somber burden of power,
> Its intolerable weight.
> He who has a heart must hear, O time,
> How your ship heads toward the depths.
>
> We have bound swallows
> Into battle legions—and now
> The sun is not visible; the entire element
> Twitters, moves, lives;
> Through the nets—dense dawn/dusk—
> The sun is not visible and the earth floats.
>
> Well, then, let's try: an enormous, clumsy,
> Creaking turn of the rudder.
> The earth floats. Courage, men.
> As with a plough, dividing the ocean,
> We will remember even in the Lethe's extreme cold,
> That the earth cost us ten heavens.

                                        (no. 103, 1917)

The Revolution

The original title, "Hymn," evokes a solemn mood reminiscent of the traditions of liturgical poetry, but it simultaneously reflects the new popular tradition of political poetry. Similarly, the first person imperative, "Let us glorify, brothers . . ." ("Proslavim, brat'ia . . ."), while emphasizing the communal nature of the speaker's vision, takes as its object of glorification the ambiguous *sumerki svobody* (dawn/dusk of freedom): *sumerki* can signify the period of semidarkness either preceding sunrise or sunset. Stanza 1 contains both meanings. While its first four lines seem to refer to "dusk," since they speak of "night waters" and "crepuscular year," its last two lines suggest dawn: "You arise in deaf, God-forsaken years, / O sun, judge, people." Images of the "sun" and the "people" were often united in popular post-Revolutionary poetry, but Mandelstam's addition of "judge" to the solemn invocation implies not only a judgment on the past, but critical prescience of the coming epoch. The opening line, then, might be interpreted ironically: we should praise what those unsympathetic to the Bolsheviks deplored as "the twilight of freedom" since their conception of "freedom" was outmoded. However, if *sumerki* refers to "dawn," it might also signify a dark, troubled time preceding the promise of the Revolution.

There is verbal tension also in the second line between the adjectives "great" and "crepuscular" that characterize the "year." While "great" continues the solemn tone of praise, "crepuscular" suggests a sense of loss and change. Is the year "great" because old prejudices are vanishing or because of expectations at the dawn of a new era? Alternative readings for *sumerki* are again possible.

The contrast between "arising" and the idea of arising "in deaf, God-forsaken years" recalls a favorite Mandelstamian subtext: Blok's poem, "Those born in the deaf, god-forsaken years / Do not remember their path / but we—children of Russia's terrible years / Cannot forget anything." The first lines of Mandelstam's autobiography, *Noise of Time,* sharply contradict them: "*I well remember* the god-forsaken years of Russia, the deaf years . . . the last refuge of a dying age." In this poem the implication that "the sun, judge, people" will "arise" amid such stagnation seems to point to *sumerki* as "dawn."

The first stanza, then, suggests not only the complexity and ambiguity of historical change, but the truly difficult task—philosophically, psychologically, and poetically—of formulating an accurate historical assessment of events.

Stanza 2 is more explicit, for the speaker identifies the object of glorification not as the new leader, but as his "burden," which implies a need for courage and help. The last lines intimate that the values of the past will sink "to the depths" to be replaced by new values, but not without loss and regret.

The third stanza is more complicated. The image of "the swallow," analogue of the human "soul" ("psyche") and the poetic "word" in *Tristia,* appears here in its folkloric meaning as harbinger of spring and renewal. Bound together in "legions," the swallows represent the Russian people as an entity, signifying that a powerful force for the future is being forged. Echoed in line four, "the entire element / Twitters,

moves, lives," we have another image of the perceived dynamism of
the Revolution.

On the other hand, the imagery of "nets" is contradictory. While
they may be related to *sumerki*—for both dim our vision and may re-
strain movement—if the Russian people-swallows are united for in-
creased strength, a positive image emerges. Also, if they are related to
the nets cast into the sea in stanza 1, and if the sea represents the sea
of life, all this may be understood positively.

Other problems suggested in stanza 3 by such negative images as
the "invisible sun," the "dense air," and the notion that the earth is
afloat, seemingly without direction, lead directly to the final stanza
and the urgent need to turn the rudder.

The colloquial appeal of the initial phrase of the concluding stanza,
"Well, then, let's try" ("Nu chto zh, poprobuem") may be in stylistic
opposition to the eloquence of "Let us glorify," but it is in keeping
with the down-to-earth emphasis on the difficulty and urgency of the
task ahead, marked by the return to high style with "Courage, men"
("Muzhajtes,' muzhi"), a possible reference to Tyutchev's ambiguous
poem, "Two voices" ("Dva golosa"), a dialogue concerning the appropriate form of "courage" required as a response to a harsh world. In
Mandelstam's poem, the new age is perceived as a period of necessity
and struggle; enthusiasm alone will hardly suffice.

The concluding lines focus on a central Mandelstamian theme: the
power of memory. Even drinking from Lethe—the netherworld's
stream of oblivion—cannot obscure the memory of the cost of "ten
heavens" incurred in the name of the new.

Ambiguity thus seems to be employed as both a poetic and polem-
ical device in opposition to the more typical Revolution poetry of blind
enthusiasm. Mandelstam's perspective is that of the present—ambivalent realism; his focus is the moment of change, the task at hand.
Doubts and misgivings arise over the burden taken on by the leader-
ship and the courage demanded of the nation. Hope depends on the
courage and endurance of the Russian people.

The Uses of the Past

Mandelstam's response to the Revolution, then, suggests both its
positive and negative potential. In 1920 Ilya Erenburg astutely noted
how unique his realism was at the time: "Poets greeted the Russian

revolution with wild shouts, hysterical tears, laments, enthusiastic frenzy, curses. But Mandelstam . . . alone understood the pathos of events."[2]

In addition to the perceptive historicism of "The Dawn/Dusk of Freedom," *Tristia* generally expresses Mandelstam's efforts to comprehend life through analogies with his literary and cultural heritage. Hence, in creating his unique mythopoetic system, he draws parallels between present and past through the inner logic of poetic association and transformation, while interpolating images and themes of Hellenism and classical mythology through the Russian neoclassical tradition.

Mandelstam's preoccupation in *Tristia* with themes of memory and recognition, with images of recurrence and repetition, metamorphosis and transformation, may be traced back to his creative reading not only of classical literature and mythology, but of Russian neoclassicism.[3] Allusions to Pushkin and Akhmatova occur with the frequency of leitmotivs. While the theme of the burden of time often appears alongside motifs of loss or fear of loss, themes and images of memory, recognition, and recurrence reinforce the idea that the ultimate challenge to time is the creative act, the preservation and promise of cultural continuity.

The poem "Tristia" (no. 104, 1918) is a fine example of the poet's endeavor to synthesize perceptions of the moment with his interpretation of "presentiments" of the past. In his essay "Word and Culture" (1921), a companion piece to *Tristia,* Mandelstam elucidates his experience of "the profound joy of recurrence" and his "recognition" of "rare presentiments," suggesting the importance of his method of textual reinterpretation for his mythopoetic system: "we have so many rare presentiments: Pushkin, Ovid, Homer. When in the stillness of the night a lover gets tangled up in tender names and suddenly remembers that all this already was: the words and the hair and the cock crowing outside his window, exactly as it had been in Ovid's *Tristia,* the profound joy of recurrence seizes him, a dizzying joy. . . ."

Victor Terras,[4] in seeking allusions to Ovid's elegy in "Tristia," has indicated how Mandelstam transformed the Latin poet's theme of parting and last "vigil"—the "last, sleepless night in his beloved Rome." If, as Terras noted, there is no cockcrow in Ovid's elegy, how does this image of "brave, pugnacious and vigilant . . . crowing" function in Mandelstam's creative reading?

Stanzas 1 and 2 juxtapose to the Ovidian lament optimistic antici-

pation "at the dawn of some new life," while stanza 3 affirms this idea
through the theme of memory and eternal recurrence clearly enunciated
in the concluding couplet.

Furthermore, the imagery of spinning and weaving that introduce
stanza 3 reinforce the bond between this stanza and Pushkin's early
creative development by emphasizing the creative process, the "verbal
fabric" of the poet's art. As V. V. Gippius, Mandelstam's former
teacher, pointed out in "Pushkin and Christianity,"[5] reading Pushkin's
early poems "Delia" and "O Delia dear" is essential to understanding
his creative evolution. Taking this one step further, we might point
out that the poet-speaker's delight in the creation of the "verbal fabric"
in "Tristia" associates Mandelstam's own poetic biography with Pushkin's. And as Terras concludes: "philosophy, art, poetry, and life itself"
are for Mandelstam "acts of anticipation, of recognition, of
rediscovery":

> I have studied the science of parting
> In the bareheaded laments of the night.
> Oxen chew, and the waiting stretches out,
> It is the last hour of the city vigils,
> And I honor the ritual of the cockerel's night,
> When, lifting their wayfarers' burden of grief,
> Tear-stained eyes peered into the distance,
> And women's weeping mingled with Muses' song.
>
> Who can know from the word parting
> What kind of separation lies ahead,
> What the cockerel's clamor promises,
> When a light burns in the acropolis,
> And at the dawn of some new life,
> When the oxen chew lazily in the stall,
> Why the cockerel, herald of the new life,
> Beats his wings on the city wall?
>
> How I love the routine of spinning:
> The shuttle's move, the spindle's hum,
> Look, how like swansdown barefoot Delia
> Already flies towards us!
> O, how meagre the basis of our life,
> How poor the language of joy!
> Everything has been, everything will recur again,
> But how sweet to us the moment of recognition.

> So be it then: a transparent figure
> Lies on a clean earthenware plate,
> Like the stretched skin of a squirrel,
> A young girl bends over the wax, gazing at it.
> Its not for us to outguess the Greek Erebus,
> Wax is for women what bronze is for men.
> Our lot falls on the battlefield only,
> But death is granted to them in divination.
>
> (no. 108, 1918)

Clarence Brown,[6] in showing how "Tristia" concerns "what the future will bring," emphasizes the Russian character of the act of divination depicted in stanza 4, for it recalls the practice of Tatyana in Pushkin's masterpiece *Eugene Onegin*: pouring melted wax into a dish of water and telling fortunes based on the solidified forms that emerge. The "stretched skin of a squirrel" refers indirectly to Akhmatova's popular poem divining the future, while "To Cassandra" (no. 95), an earlier *Tristia* poem dedicated to Akhmatova, also associates her with divination. Hence, Mandelstam's synthesis of "presentiments," allusions, and memories, his creative rereading of cultural texts, act "to ease the burden of time" by challenging Ovid's elegiac voice and emphasizing cultural continuity.

The Myth of St. Petersburg

The patterns of image formation and transformation that unite the philosophical, psychological, and poetic ambivalence of "The Dawn/ Dusk of Freedom" with the poetics of cultural continuity expressed in "Tristia" are connected through Mandelstam's St. Petersburg myth.

The St. Petersburg myth is developed through two closely related patterns. The first evokes the contrast between the cold, dark, northern capital and the world of sunlight, the latter being associated with the south, the Crimea, the Black Sea, and, by extension, the entire Mediterranean world. The sources of beauty and culture associated with classical antiquity, Hellenism, and Judeo-Christian tradition are reflected in this pattern.[7]

The pattern of contrast is elucidated in two poems of 1917: no. 92, "The stream of golden honey flowed from the bottle" ("Zolotistogo meda struia . . .") and no. 93, "Still far away the transparent-grey spring of asphodels" ("Eshche daleko asfodelei . . ."). The latter draws a direct contrast between St. Petersburg and the Crimea, a motif continued and expanded two years later in such poems as no. 105, "On the rocky spurs of Pieria" ("Na kamennykh otrogakh Pierii"), and no. 106, "What steepness in the crystal pool" ("V khrustal'nom omute . . ."). In the second poem, Christian motifs and images are introduced and the geographical range is extended from the Siennese hills to Palestine. This same pattern is further developed and transformed more than a decade later in *Journey to Armenia.*

The second, and by far the stronger, pattern—invoking the Persephone myth—first emerges in two pre-Revolutionary poems of 1916 derived from a single verbal and thematic impulse: no. 88, "I'm cold. Transparent spring / Dresses Petropolis in green down" ("Mne kholodno. Prozrachnaia vesna"), and no. 89, "In transparent Petropolis we will die" ("V Petropole prozrachnom my umrem"). Tangentially, it also occurs in no. 87, "—I lost my dear cameo . . . on the Neva shore" ("Ia poterialo nezhnuiu kameiu . . ."), and again in 1917 in no. 95, "To Cassandra" ("Kassandre"). Poeticized here as "Petropolis," St. Petersburg refers not only to the contemporary city but symbolizes the cultural legacy of Derzhavin and Pushkin.

In stark opposition to the celebratory image of St. Petersburg portrayed in *Stone,* "Transparent Petropolis" now emerges as a cold, dark, northern city through which runs the threatening Neva River, emblematic of anxiety, loss, and disgust:

> In Transparent Petropolis We Will Die
>
> In transparent Petropolis we will die
> Where Proserpina rules over us.
> In every breath we drink the deathly air,
> And each hour for us is the hour of death.
> Goddess from the sea, awesome Athena,
> Remove your mighty stone helmet.
> In transparent Petropolis we will die
> For not you, but Proserpina, reigns here.
> (no. 89, 1916)

Mandelstam's mythopoetic association of the Persephone myth with St. Petersburg is first made here. Persephone emphasizes duality, for in addition to presiding over the "transparent" souls of the dead, she is a harbinger of spring and renewal, representing the natural cycle of seasonal change. Condemned to spend part of the year in the underworld with her husband, Hades, the rest of the year she may freely ascend to earth to live with her mother, Demeter, goddess of fertility.

Mandelstam's choice of the Persephone myth at this juncture functions both to reinforce his own ambivalent worldview and to expand his poetics of cultural continuity. The connection between Proserpina-Persephone's "transparent" world of shades and St. Petersburg-Petropolis is explicit. The reference to Athena, goddess of wisdom and mercy, alludes to her stone statue in the vestibule of the Admiralty, located on the Neva embankment; hence, "stone helmet" and "from the sea." Athena's powers, however, have been usurped by the underworld queen.

Although no. 88, "I'm cold. Transparent spring / Dresses Petropolis in green down," begins with the speaker's anticipation of spring, the tone shifts in the middle of the first quatrain after the conjunction "but" and the acknowledgment of "disgust" at the "Neva's wave." The sestet reiterates the pattern. However, the imagery evoked in its first four lines is diffused by the repetition of "but" and a parallel antithesis: "no stars can kill / The sea wave's heavy emerald," which is far more poignant than "slight disgust":

> I'm Cold. Transparent Spring
>
> I'm cold. Transparent spring
> Dresses Petropolis in green down.
> But, like a medusa, the Neva's wave
> Fills me with slight disgust.
> Along the quay of the northern river
> Fireflies of automobiles rush past,
> Dragonflies and beetles of steel fly,
> And the golden pins of stars flicker,
> But no stars can kill
> The sea wave's heavy emerald.
>   (no. 88, 1916)

The epithet "transparent," then, comes to represent the theme of memento mori, while the Neva, like a Styx of the upper world, threatens the world of St. Petersburg and Russian culture.

In the first stanza of no. 101, "At a terrifying height . . ." ("Na strashnoi vysote . . ."), a poem dating from 1918, an unidentified flying object is sighted as some kind of "transparent star" or "wandering fire." As "Petropolis' brother," it implies the form Petropolis will take after its imminent descent into the netherworld. Combined with the epithet "terrifying," which opens each of the first three stanzas, it amounts to a haunting omen of death. The poem thus quite explicitly

expresses Mandelstam's doubts about the future of St. Petersburg and
Russia's cultural heritage:

> At a Terrifying Height a Wandering Fire
>
> At a terrifying height a wandering fire,
> But does a star twinkle like this?
> Transparent star, wandering fire,
> Your brother, Petropolis, is dying.
>
> At a terrifying height earthly dreams burn,
> A green star flies.
> Oh, if you are a star, the brother of water and sky,
> Your brother, Petropolis, is dying.
>
> A monstrous ship at a terrifying height
> Is speeding, spreading its wings—
> Green star, in beautiful poverty
> Your brother, Petropolis, is dying.
>
> Transparent spring over the black Neva
> Has shattered, the wax of immortality melts,
> Oh, if you are a star, Petropolis, your city,
> Your brother, Petropolis, is dying.
>   (no. 101, 1918; trans. Broyde)[8]

Several obvious self-quotations appear here from the poems of 1916
and from *Stone*. For instance, viewing the "transparent star" as a
"brother to sky and sea" and a "monstrous ship . . . speeding," recall
the Admiralty spire with its ship weathervane, emblematic in "The
Admiralty" of St. Petersburg's positive, forward-looking vision. Similarly, the epithet "green" recalls the portrayal of the Admiralty as "lost
among the leaves, / And through the dark green a frigate or acropolis /
Gleams in the distance, brother to sky and sea."

In "At a terrifying height," however, the celebratory tonality of *Stone*
has vanished. Most significant, perhaps, both the Admiralty itself and
the poem in its honor no longer symbolize creation or the connection
with the world of Western culture. The Admiralty, with its now "monstrous" ship, emerges as a reflection of dying St. Petersburg-Petropolis.
Only St. Petersburg's dual nature—barely suggested in the earlier
poem when it is described as a northern city "open to the seas of the
world"—is greatly expanded in *Tristia*.

"At a terrifying height" is related more indirectly to "Petersburg Stanzas," a montage of themes associated with Russian history and culture—literary references to Gogol and Pushkin, historical references to the Decembrist revolt of 1825 and to the contemporary city. "Petersburg Stanzas" also portray the Neva and the Admiralty, but very positively: "The Neva has embassies from half the globe, / The sun, the Admiralty, and silence." What is more, the fact that St. Petersburg is a northern city has no negative connotations. There is a sense of pervasive tranquility:

> Steamers are moored until spring. Where the sun
> Is hot, the thick glass of cabin windows glows.
> Russia, like some enormous dreadnaught,
> Lies at her dock in ponderous repose.

Mandelstam's self-reminiscences to *Stone,* then, emphasize his transformed, mythopoetic vision of the former cultural capital of the Russian empire.

The concluding stanza of "At a Terrifying Height" contains another self-quotation when it refers to the "wax of immortality" melting. By suggesting the process of divination cited in "Tristia," this image may imply that the fate of St. Petersburg is being decided; but if "Petropolis is dying," the future looks bleak. In addition to suggesting that St. Petersburg, and with it Russia's cultural heritage, is dying, this poem attains greater power through Mandelstam's intense psychological bonding of the city with his own destiny: he fears that his personal and poetic biography might vanish with it.

No. 118, "We will gather again in Petersburg" ("V Peterburge my soidemsia snova"), is far more complex than nos. 88, 89, or 101, constructed as it is through semantic associations, cultural reminiscences, and a strict inner logic. Unlike the above or other poems from 1920 (nos. 112–114), allusions to the "transparent" world or the dark Neva, or to signs, divination, and December are absent. Nevertheless, the speaker's assertion that "we will meet again in Petersburg" for the purpose of performing a requiem to venerate the "buried sun" links this poem with the Petersburg-Persephone myth and reflects Mandelstam's concern over the fate of Russia's cultural heritage, for the requiem will be performed in St. Petersburg. The scene is a cold "January" or "Soviet" night (depending on the edition of the poem);[9] a theater performance is coming to a close. The contemporary city, portrayed in stanza two, is compared to a "wild cat" poised to leap. The image of the car "tearing through the gloom" recalls similar imagery in "I'm cold. Transparent spring," and its crying "like a cuckoo" suggests mournfulness. Topical details include "sentries" and "night passes":

We will gather again in Petersburg,
As if we had buried the sun there,
And the blessed messageless word
We will utter for the first time.
In the black velvet of the Soviet/January night,
In the velvet of universal emptiness
Kindred eyes of blessed women still sing,
Immortal flowers still bloom.

The capital arches like a wild cat,
A patrol stands on the bridge,
Now and then a ferocious car tears by in the gloom,
And cries out like a cuckoo.
I don't need a night pass,
I don't fear the sentries:
For the blessed messageless word
I will pray in the Soviet/January night.
I hear a light theater rustle,
And a girl sighing "ah"—
And a huge bunch of immortal roses
In Cypris' arms.
We warm ourselves by the fire from boredom,
Ages, perhaps, will pass,
And the dear hands of the blessed women
Will gather the light ashes.

Somewhere the red flowerbeds of the parterre,
The chiffoniers of the loges are luxuriously fluffed up;
The clockwork doll of an officer;
Not for black souls and base hypocrites . . .
Well, blow out our candles
In the black velvet of universal emptiness,
Rounded shoulders of the blessed women still sing,
And you will not notice the night sun.
                        (no. 118, November 25, 1920; trans. Broyde,
                                                           adapted)

Nevertheless, the ominous atmosphere in which the speaker contemplates the requiem is imbued with the poet's fearless faith in the immortality of beauty, art, and poetry. He seems to assume his fellow Acmeists will attend and gather the ashes of Pushkin and Russia's cultural legacy so as to venerate them; that the buried poet will be honored with new poetry, for as Acmeists, the poetic word will be uttered as if "for the first time." Moreover, he expresses faith that there will always be "immortal flowers" and that "blessed women" will continue to venerate the "blessed, messageless word." The speaker even says he "will pray for the blessed, messageless word," the pure poetic word, explained as nonutilitarian, nonobligatory, and compared to a "soul" or "psyche" in "Word and Culture": "The life of the word has entered a heroic era. . . . Do not demand from poetry any special substantiality, materiality, or concreteness. . . . why equate the word with the thing, with grass, with the object it designates. . . . The word is Psyche" (*CPL*, 115).

The "sun" image is explained in detail in "Pushkin and Scriabin":

Pushkin and Scriabin, two transformations of the same sun . . . served as an example of a collective Russian death. . . .

Pushkin was buried at night . . . secretly. . . . The sun was placed in its coffin at night, and the sled runners scraped the frozen January ground as they bore the poet's remains away for the funeral.

I recall this picture of Pushkin's funeral so as to arouse in your memory the image of the night sun, the image of Euripides' last Greek tragedy—the vision of ill-fated Phaedra. (*CPL*, 90)

Hence, the imagined requiem for Pushkin is compared to a dramatic performance of a Greek tragedy, perhaps Euripides' *Phaedra*, in which the "blessed women" enact the chorus. This poem is thus connected with Mandelstam's motif of the St. Petersburg theater, always associated with tragic and beloved women (see nos. 81–82, 119–20, or 122).

The last stanza, however ambiguous, also seems to affirm the theme of continuity and immortality. The affirmative nature of the poem's opening line takes the form of a challenge in the last line, if it is read to mean that those who blow out candles "will not notice" how the cultural tradition is preserved even in periods of "universal emptiness," regardless of history and time. The "night sun"—Pushkin, poetry— will shine despite the "black velvet of the January/Soviet night." [10]

Again Mandelstam's ambivalence emerges, although the complex of images—blessed women, kindred eyes, rounded shoulders, immortal flowers, Cypris, roses, and the blessed, messageless word—suggesting the immortality of love, beauty, and poetry as the ultimate challenge to history, time, and change, support an optimistic reading of this text.

Words, Sounds, and Poetic Creation

The last poem to be considered in this chapter—no. 113, "I have forgotten the word I wanted to say" ("Ia slovo pozabyl, chto ia khotel skazat'")—was written in November 1920, the same month as "We will gather again in Petersburg." In that it treats the fundamental problem of poetic creation and cultural memory through the Persephone myth, it may be read as the culmination of the major lyric impulse behind *Tristia*.

Both the real and the imagined experience of fear of muteness function in this poem as a creative impulse. According to Akhmatova, Mandelstam "feared his own muteness, calling it asphyxia. When it gripped him, he rushed about in terror."[11] Mandelstam's anxiety, however, was not simply over personal fear of loss, but fear for the loss of cultural memory, fear for "the word" as a vehicle of cultural continuity.

Hence, the "blind swallow with clipped wings" metaphorically represents the unexpressed and potentially inexpressible poetic "word" so intimately connected with the poet's intense fear of the loss of creative power. The "return" of the "swallow"/soul/"word" to the "hall of shades," where all is incorporeal, mute, and dry, is his ultimate nightmare:

I have forgotten the word I wanted to say.
A blind swallow with clipped wings returns
To the hall of shades to play with the transparent ones.
The night song is sung in obliviousness.

No sound of birds. No blooms on the immortelle.
The manes of the night herd are transparent.
An empty boat floats in a dry river.
Amidst the crickets the word lies oblivious.

It rises slowly like a tent or temple,
Then suddenly feigns the mad Antigone,
Then flings itself at their feet, like a dead swallow
With Stygian tenderness and a green branch.

Oh, if only the shame of seeing fingers could return
And the wide-eyed joy of recognition.
How fearful I am of the Aonides weeping,
Of the mist, the ringing, and the yawning gulf.

Power is given to mortals to love and to recognize,
Sound also will pour into their fingers,
But I forgot what I wanted to say,
The unembodied thought will return to the hall of shades.

Again and again the transparent one just repeats:
The swallow, friend, Antigone. . . .
But like black ice on my lips
Burns the memory of the Stygian tolling.

                                         (no. 113, November 1920)

This poem, however, provides us with a poetic paradox, for "the word" is recollected, the poem written. Mandelstam's most negative theme—fear of muteness—yields a rich modernist text, a description of the act of recollection by way of the Persephone myth.

The poem's plot, based on the internal logic of association rather than on objective narrative, depicts the act of recollection through an imagined journey of "the word" down to the river Styx, vicariously experienced by the poet-persona. The imagined journey includes tentative attempts on the part of "the word" to return to the world of mortals, the bearing of mortal gifts to the shades, and the poet-speaker's own feelings of loss, intense yearning and awe-filled terror. The poet's consciousness, his inner experience of fear, provides the encompassing framework. The poem ends, paradoxically, on a positive note, in that the speaker's vicarious journey has left him with so strong an impression that it resembles "black ice" burning his "lips." That is, although his imaginary experience and the recollection of that experience were terrifyingly "black," his creative powers—his "lips"—were stimulated. Both the imagined fear and its memory function as the impulse behind this highly original text.

Even though Mandelstam's subject is frightening, the poem is death-defying. Indeed, it is in this poem that Mandelstam recognizes explicitly what he intimates in much of *Tristia,* that the source of poetry may just as likely be "winter and night" as spring and sunlight, a concept developed further in *Noise of Time* and *1921–1925.* Nor was this idea new to Mandelstam, for as early as 1908, in his letter to

V. V. Gippius, he noted his attraction to the early symbolists' "ingenious boldness of negation, pure negation."

Another remarkable aspect of "I have forgotten the word" is its vivid, almost tangible portrayal of the netherworld. Although presented primarily through negative images, images of absence ("No sound of birds. No blooms on the immortelles"); it is a place where the "transparent ones" dwell, the netherworld is concretized. In contrast, the world of mortals is evoked only through its ideals—"power is given to mortals to love and to recognize"—and through the speaker's intense yearning for mortal life: "Oh, if only the shame of seeing fingers could return / And the wide-eyed joy of recognition." Thus, the distinctions the poet draws between the world of mortals and the world of shades are not so much between life and death as between an active emotional life and passive, suspended existence.

Through the device of contrast and juxtaposition, this poem attempts to avoid the problem expressed by the poet-speaker in "Tristia": "How poor the language of joy!" Indeed, the juxtaposition of the concretely visual world of the shades and the inner world of human emotions and ideals is extremely effective, as is the contrast between the states of mind vicariously experienced by the poet's "I" as he variously imagines "the word" as "blind swallow," "oblivious word," and "unembodied thought."

"The word" is first imagined as a "blind swallow / soul on clipped wings" descending to visit and play with the "transparent ones." At the lowest point in its passive, suspended existence it is portrayed in a state of "obliviousness." Finally, in stanza 3, "the word" is imagined desperately fighting for life, trying to "rise" up out of the netherworld, first by "feigning Antigone" (that is, showing tenderness toward the souls of the dead), then by acting like a "dead swallow / soul" attempting to assuage the shades with offerings, first "Stygian tenderness," then a "green branch," a token of "life." Finally, in stanza 5, "the word" is again conceived as "incorporeal," as "unembodied thought."

Simultaneously, the poet-speaker's own passionate yearning for the full emotional experience of life on earth, his subsequent comprehension of "the power granted to mortals to love and to recognize," and his extreme sensitivity to the sounds of the underworld, coalesce into his poignant and painful "memory" of "Stygian tolling," the incessant sounding of which impelled its transformation into verse.

Equally significant, the poem's phonic devices reiterate its thematic paradox. The contrast between the sounds of the upper world, depicted as the absence of earthly sounds—"No birds sing"—and the fearful sounds of the underworld—the Muses' weeping and Stygian tolling—is emphasized at the end of the second stanza by the phrase "the word becomes oblivious" / "without memory" (*bes*pamiatstvuet sl*ov*o). The dominant stanzaic position of this phrase makes it a kind of summary of the first two stanzas. The Russian words may be translated either as "obliviousness" or "memorylessness." In its state of "memorylessness," "the word" fully echoes the "night song" of Hades: "The night song is sung in obliviousness / memorylessness" (v *bes*pamiatstve).

Mandelstam's interest in phonic play and juxtaposition does not end here. We can observe how this state of "oblivion," representing the lowest point in the descent of "the word" (only in stanza 3 does it attempt to rise), is contrasted through phonic juxtaposition with the poem's concluding line, in which the poet's "memory" so haunts him. The poem's concluding words, placed in the strongest position in the text, read: "the recollection / memory of the tolling" (*vos*pominane z*vo*na).

Highly significant here is the phonemic transformation, the reversal of the central syllables of "sl*ov*a" (the word) into "z*vo*na" (the sound), aided by the obvious (to a Russian ear) opposition between prefixes, the negative "bes-" (without, loss of), and the positive "vos-" ("re"—as in *re*surrect, "up"—as in raise *up*), implying a significant reversal in the poet-persona's psychological state, and affirming the poet's recollection/memory of "the word." The subsequent exchange of "word" (sl*ov*o) and "sound" (z*vo*n-a) occurs because the memory of the tolling stimulates the poet's powers and moves his lips, transforming his experience into art—the "sound" becomes the "word." The poem's phonic structure thus reinforces its paradoxical theme, and indeed generates its optimistic conclusion.

Hence, Mandelstam's philosophical, psychological, and poetic ambivalence as reflected in his mythopoesis, his simultaneous attraction to both life and death as expressed through the Persephone myth, his impulse to express life's burdens as well as its joys, his recognition of the need for courage and strength as well as his acknowledgment of fear and trembling, determine the thematics, tonality, imagery, semantics, and even the phonic basis of *Tristia,* a collection that ultimately proves that for Mandelstam the negative creative impulse can serve as a challenge to time and as a source of cultural continuity.

Chapter Four
Noise of Time

My desire is to speak not about myself but to track down the age, the noise
and the germination of time . . .

Noise of Time, (1923–25)

Autobiography, History, and Myth

Noise of Time (*Shum vremeni*), Mandelstam's lyrical autobiography, initiates a new phase in the poet's creative work. Not only does he use his
own life as basic poetic material for the first time, but he chooses to
shape his autobiographical myth in terms of Russia's cultural history,
linking his "literary genesis" with the history of the age in which he
grew up.

In his essay "End of the Novel" ("Konets romana"), conceived within
a few years of the autobiography, Mandelstam noted that the "pivot"
of the nineteenth-century novel was "human biography"—the "sense
of time man possesses to act, to conquer, to perish and to love. . . ."
Simultaneously, however, he indicated his fear that twentieth-century
man was "devoid of biography." Hence, the poet had no choice but to
dismiss the novel as a viable genre in seeking an appropriate form to
examine his own "sense of time" as a man *and* as a poet. What is more,
Noise of Time also rejects the nineteenth-century genres of self-reflexive
prose because, as Mandelstam claimed in the programmatic statement
to that work, there was nothing more than a "hiatus" in his biography
where a traditional family history "ought to have been."

In Mandelstam's programmatic statement—which opens the penultimate chapter of *Noise of Time*—the primacy of memoir is established
and emphasized, the presentation of the self placed in the historical
context. In addition, it is here that Mandelstam defines his concern for
his "literary genesis" as opposed to his family heritage. He does so by
continuing the thematic impulse of *Tristia,* declaring the negative impulses of his memory significant sources of inspiration, and by rejecting outright a self-image based on the "personal" or familial.

The object of Mandelstam's autobiography, then, became the recovery of a "sense of time" through the association of his individual destiny with Russia's cultural history. As a man "devoid of biography," he had first to comprehend the epoch that influenced his formative years and only then to define his self-image in history. As a poet, he had to acquire a language to articulate that history, for his was to be an act of cultural memory, a biography created out of history and literature, not a story of the development of an individual's inner psyche. Consciousness of personal identity came only after the Revolution—and as a result of it—with its sudden illumination of Russia's historical and cultural traditions, and with the poet's consequent identification of personal, aesthetic, and intellectual developments with Russia's cultural heritage. Mandelstam's programmatic statement reads:

My desire is to speak *not about myself* but to *track down the age, the noise, and the germination of time.* My memory is inimical to all that is personal. *If* it depended on *me,* I should only make a wry face in remembering the past. I was never able to understand the Tolstoys and Aksakovs . . . enamoured of family archives . . . I repeat—my labor is not to reproduce but *to distance the past.* A *raznochinets* needs no memory—it is enough for him to tell of the books he has read, and his biography is done. Where for happy generations the epic speaks in hexameters and chronicles, I have merely the sign of the *hiatus,* and *between me and the age there lies an abyss,* a moat filled with clamorous time, the place where a family and reminiscences of *family ought to have been.* What was it my family wished to say? I do not know. It was tongue-tied from birth— *but* it had, nevertheless, *something it might have said.* Over my head and that of many of my contemporaries hangs congenital tongue-tie. We were not taught to speak but to babble—and *only by listening to the swelling noise of the age* and the bleached foam on the crest of its wave *did we acquire a language.* (109–10; *SS,* 2:99)[1]

Since Mandelstam sought and found the source of his consciousness in neither his inner psyche nor his family, but in history and "the books he had read," he came to identify his adult self-image as that of a "*raznochinets*-writer," a critical intellectual with leanings toward the fourth estate seeking his roots in Russia's cultural history. Indeed, he sought his "literary genesis" in "the bookcase of early childhood": "The bookcase of early childhood is a *man's companion* for life. . . . There was nothing haphazard in the way that strange little library had been deposited, like a *geological bed,* over decades. The paternal and maternal elements were not mixed, but existed separately, and a cross-section of the strata showed the *history of the spiritual efforts of the entire family*, as well as the inoculation of it with *alien blood*" (78; *SS*, 2:57).

Mandelstam eventually substituted Russian writers and literature for his own family. He imagined his teacher, V. V. Gippius, as the source of literature, and his home as "literature's own house":

I would come to him [Gippius] to wake up the beast of literature. . . . *I would come to my teacher of Russian at home.* The whole savor of the thing lay in that coming to him "at home." *Even now* it is difficult for me to free myself from *the notion that I was then at literature's own house.* . . .

Beginning as early as Radishchev and Novikov, V. V. had established *personal relations with Russian writers,* splenetic and loving liaisons filled with noble enviousness, jealousy, with jocular disrespect, grievous unfairness—*as is customary between the members of a family.* . . . V. V.'s judgments continue to hold me to this day. . . . (115–16; *SS*, 2:106)

Structural Elements

To understand Mandelstam's autobiography more fully, it is essential to examine its structural elements and the means by which his philosophical, historical, and aesthetic ideas are incorporated into the text. First of all, the opening phrase, "I well remember . . ." immediately initiates the reader into the poet's autobiographical task by affirming the power of memory and relating it to historical consciousness. The personal experience is established as part of a given historical context.

Second, the reader is alerted that a significant element of aesthetic coherence in this text derives from the juxtaposition of historical details—visualized "in scenes"—and aural images, "noises of time," historical undercurrents associated with music and performances:

I well remember the god-forsaken years of Russian, the deaf years, the decade of the nineties. . . . At morning tea there would be talk about Dreyfus, there were *the names* of Colonels Esterhazy and Picquart, vague disputes about some "Kreutzer Sonata" and, *behind the high podium* of the glass railroad station in Pavlovsk, *the change of conductors* which seemed to me a *change of dynasties* . . . and, all in all, *I picture* the nineties . . . *in scenes* scattered apart but *inwardly bound* together by the quiet misery and the painful, doomed provincialism of the life that was dying. (69; *SS*, 2:45)

Third, the autobiographical narrator initiates the reader into his faith in the "word" as a vehicle of cultural memory, emphasizing that his experience is of memory and history, for his autobiographical imagination restructures experience by subjecting it to aesthetic interpretation. For example, the immediacy of the child-hero's first memories—a precise historical occasion—is mediated through the adult narrator's retrospective transformation of those "perceptions" into "spectacle": "My first conscious sharp perceptions were of gloomy crowds of people in the streets. I was exactly three years old. It was 1894 and I had been brought from Pavlovsk to Petersburg for the purpose of seeing the funeral of Alexander III. . . . having crawled up on the windowsill and seen the crowd-darkened street, I asked, 'When will they start?' and was told 'tomorrow'" (75; *SS*, 2:53).

Even more telling, Mandelstam's final chapter proposes the art of retrospection as the only path for comprehending the present:

> To remember not living people but plaster casts struck from their voices. To go blind. *To feel and recognize by hearing.* Sad fate! *Thus does one penetrate into the present,* into the *modern age,* as via the bed of a dried up river.
>
> As you know, those were not friends, nor near ones, but alien, distant people! *Still, it is only* with the masks of other men's voices that the bare walls of my house are decorated. *To remember*—to make one's way alone back up the dried riverbed!
>
> The first literary encounter is irremediable. . . . (113; *SS*, 2:104)

Noise of Time is thus unique in that historical data and aesthetically conceived events are poetically transformed to create, rather than re-create, the life of the hero out of Russia's cultural history. A proliferation of accurate historical names, places, and events—historical nomenclature—helps create a self-image in which a vivid historical context enriches the personal and a concrete physiological reality engenders the spiritual. Mandelstam's attempt gradually to identify the destiny of his autobiographical hero with Russia's cultural destiny, with Russian history, derives from his conviction that the Russian language *is* Russian history. This conviction is associated with his interest in Bergson, first enunciated in his essay "On the Nature of the Word."

Bergson's theory of time as duration (*la durée*), as Mandelstam interpreted it, was concerned not merely with the operation of the individual psyche, but with the enduring self "in its flowing through time," that is, the self in history. In his *Introduction to Metaphysics,* Bergson stated: "There is one reality, at least, which we all seize from within, by intuition and not by simple analysis. It is our personality in its flowing through time—our self which endures."[2] Mandelstam's theoretical reformulation of this idea, his conceptualization and literary expression of the "awareness of experience as continuous process," was not fully realized until he wrote *Conversation about Dante* ten years later. In that work he declared: "poetic material . . . exists only in performance . . . [the] finished poem is no more than . . . the inevitable result of the impulse to perform." However, *Noise of Time* may be read as an early effort to create that same sense of "performance" or continuous process by using the open prose genre of autobiography rather than the closed forms of lyric poetry that dominated his creative work until 1923. The hero's developing aesthetic consciousness is thus revealed *in process*, "in performance," as the memorable moments of the poet's life and of Russia's history are filtered through the hero's growing poetic imagination.

In "On the Nature of the Word," which preceded *Noise of Time* by one year, Mandelstam cited Bergson as he attempted to comprehend the "nature" and "source" of "the word," in particular, the "Russian literary language," which he goes so far as to equate with Russian history: "so highly organized, so organic a language is not merely a door into history, but *is history itself*." What is more, he even tells the reader why he perceives the Russian language as "historical": "the Russian language is historical by its very nature, since in its totality it is a turbulent sea of events, a continuous incarnation and activation of rational and breathing flesh" (*CPL* 121; *SS,* 2:246). The poet's task, then, as Mandelstam perceives it, is the articulation of Russian history. He takes this notion one step further in his autobiography, where he depicts his own "personality in its flowing through time . . .," thus expressing Russian history through his autobiographical myth. In this way, *Noise of Time* articulates Mandelstam's philosophical conception of the poet's intuitive grasp of time, specifically, the fluid quality of reality, the awareness of experience as continuous process, in keeping with his reading of Bergson and his reformulation of Acmeist poetics in "On the Nature of the Word."

Mandelstam's strategy of parallelism is introduced to the reader gradually as the chronological phases of the autobiography unfold, concretizing the poet's intuitive sense of self by portraying its integral relationship to the flow of time—of Russian cultural history. The autobiographer's intense interest in the historical theme elevates it to a structural level in his text parallel to the anticipated psychophysiological theme of nineteenth-century autobiography. In addition, Mandelstam's aesthetic doctrine "not to reproduce but to distance the past" superimposes an aesthetic dimension on his treatment of time consciousness. The theme of aesthetic consciousness is thereby elevated to a structural level parallel to the themes of historical and psychophysiological consciousness.

The parallels presented in Mandelstam's autobiography include (1) the periods of historical consciousness: 1890s, 1900s, and post-Revolutionary Russia; (2) the stages of psychophysiological growth of the protagonist marked by the imagery of music: childhood (Tchaikovsky's *1812 Overture*), adolescence (Tchaikovsky's *Symphonie Pathetique* and the concerts of Hoffman and Kubelik), and maturity (poetry, marked by the refrain "Sing, Mary," in his version of Pushkin's *Feast During the Plague*); (3) the phases of aesthetic consciousness: "political aesthetics," "the aesthetic of the intellect," and the aesthetic of conscience, "literary savagery"; and (4) the types of literature associated with each aesthetic-historical epoch expressed through the symbolics of literary performance: the literature of reflection ("Nadsonism" and the Literary Fund); the literature of disengagement (symbolism); and "serious Russian literature," or the literature of conscience (Pushkin's *Feast During the Plague*).

Childhood

The narrative structure of *Noise of Time* emerges from the gradual identification of the hero's consciousness with the historical periods under discussion. These periods correspond to the stages of the hero's psychophysiological growth, which in turn correspond to the phases of aesthetic consciousness first experienced by the narrator-hero and then recalled and reimagined by the poet-autobiographer. The literary reminiscences that metaphorically reiterate the process of aesthetic-historical change are singled out by the autobiographical narrator as links between the personal, historical, and aesthetic layers of this work, for they reflect the stages of the poet-hero's "literary genesis." Moreover, the literary references are all to "performances" and hence suggest the as yet unformulated concept expressed later in *Conversation about Dante* that "poetry exists only in performance." In the autobiography, aesthetic consciousness is represented as in process. *Noise of Time,* then, may perhaps be read as poetry in the process of formation, as a prose poem "in performance."

Some examples may be offered here. As the reader is carefully guided into the period of the 1890s by the autobiographical narrator, he first perceives the epoch through the mind of the narrator-protagonist or child-hero. The reader gradually realizes that the child's subjective perspective on this period in Russian history is identical with the mature autobiographical narrator's distant retrospective evaluation. In a word, the epoch itself is judged as "Childhood" to the "Adolescence" of Russia's 1900s and to the "Maturity" of post-Revolutionary Russia. To illustrate this point, we may note that while the aesthetic consciousness of the period is defined as "police aesthetics" from the narrator's retrospective vision, the vitality of the age is illuminated by the child's subjective views on growing up in Russia's cultural capital:

> All this mass of militarism and even a kind of *police esthetics* may very well have been *proper* to some son of a corps commander with *appropriate* family traditions, *but*. . . .
> The Petersburg street *awakened in me a craving for spectacle,* and the very architecture of the city *inspired me* with a kind of *childish imperialism.*
> Even *death first appeared to me* in a totally *unnatural, elegant and festive guise.* (74; *SS,* 2:52)

Furthermore, the "police esthetics" of the 1890s which so enthrall the child, are offered to the reader as the dominant aesthetic value of the period, just as the most popular reading matter—the fantastic "miscellanies"—indicates that the interests and values of the child are "identical" with the spirit of the age, with the interests and values of the adults: "I loved the 'miscellany' about ostrich eggs, two-headed calves, and festivals in Bombay and Calcutta, and especially the huge, full-page pictures: Malayan swimmers . . . the mysterious experiment of a M. Fouque . . . *I have a feeling that the grown ups read the same thing as I,* that is, mainly the immense, burgeoning supplements to *The Field* and the rest. *Our interests were, in general, identical* . . . at seven or eight I was *fully abreast* of the age . . ." (70; *SS,* 2:47). In this way, historical and aesthetic consciousness of the 1890s emerges through the eyes and mind of the child-hero, who in turn reflects Russia's own "Childhood" from the autobiographical narrator's post-Revolutionary perspective.

It is not surprising, then, that this entire epoch is characterized by childishness, frivolity, naiveté, and tranquil pleasures, on the one hand, and by its "deafness" to the undercurrents of ideological, economic, and social change on the other. The imagery of the period establishes its superficiality and artificiality while alluding to its external harmony, visual beauty, and architecture as "childish imperialism." All this is opposed to the undercurrents of dissonance, discord, and confusion that characterize the coming age of "Adolescence,"marked by heightened aural and musical imagery. The intellectuals of the 1890s are presented as visually acute, but deaf, for these are the "deaf years of Russia, the decade of the nineties."

Hence, the perception of the 1890s as the "Childhood" of contemporary Russian history derives from autobiographical retrospection, engendered by Mandelstam's recognition and acceptance of the Revolution as the catastrophic event which, ironically perhaps, made comprehension of pre-Revolutionary Russia possible, and consequently inspired him to write his autobiography, thus preserving its memory. On the last page of the text, the autobiographer—now the mature *"raznochinets*-writer" living in the new, intensely historically conscious age—clarifies his aesthetic revelation: "Looking back at the entire nineteenth century of Russian culture—shattered, finished, unrepeatable, which no one should repeat, which no one dares repeat—I wish to hail the century, as one would hail settled weather. I see in it the unity lent it by the measureless cold which welded decades together into one day, one night, one profound winter, within which the terrible State glowed, like a stove, in ice" (117; *SS*, 2:108).

The reader is thus introduced simultaneously to the first period of the autobiographer's life experience, "Childhood," and to the earliest sources of his awakening historical and aesthetic consciousness. Furthermore, the subjective childhood experience is both objectified through the *"raznochinets*-writer's" memory of nineteenth-century Russia, and aestheticized through his new poetics of conscience and challenge, "literary savagery." The hero's and the author's personal experience is identified metaphorically with Russia's history. In interpreting the "noise of time," therefore, the *"raznochinets"*-autobiographer speaks as its bard.

Adolescence

A similar case can be made for the correlation of the second phase of the narrator's life experience, the period of "Adolescence," with Russia's 1900s, and for the correlation of "Maturity" or "Adulthood" with the post-Revolutionary years, the time when the autobiography was composed.

From the retrospective viewpoint of the autobiographical narrator, adolescence intensified and further defined his aesthetic and historical consciousness, paving the way for their eventual and, in Mandelstam's post-Revolutionary view, inevitable synthesis.

In contrast to the 1890s, marked by "police esthetics," the 1900s were a time of the "esthetic of the intellect," portrayed through the adolescent hero's friendship with Boris Sinani and his family: "The central feature of the Sinani household was what I should call *an esthetic of the intellect.* Positivism is usually hostile to esthetic contemplation, the disinterested pride and joy of the movements of the mind. But for these people the intellect was joy, health, sport and almost religion, all at once." (105; *SS,* 2:93).

"Adolescence" is marked by the intensity of the young hero's responses to music in conjunction with his psychophysiological identification with the power of art. The intensity of his response to music also indicates that neither he nor the 1900s in general were "deaf" to the anxiety and agitation of the age: "At this time I conceived for Tchaikovsky a painfully nervous and intense love that recalled the desire of Dostoevsky's Netochka Nezvanovna to hear the violin concert behind the red flame of the silk curtains. . . . I heard from behind a barbed-wire fence [in Jewish Dubbeln the orchestra strained at Tchaikovsky's *Symphonie Pathetique*] and more than once I tore my clothes and covered my hands with scratches as I made my way gratis to the orchestra shell. . . . What a thread it is that runs from these first wretched concerts to the silk flame of Nobility Hall . . ." (87–88; *SS,* 2:70).

The intensity of the adolescent perspective, then, reflects the heightened historical and ideological consciousness of the immediate pre-Revolutionary years, expressed everywhere but marked especially in this work in the concert halls, where art alone has the power to control imminent catastrophe:

In the season of 1903–04 Petersburg witnessed concerts in the grand manner . . . the concerts of Hofmann and Kubelik in the Nobility Hall during Lent . . . would reach a kind of rage, a fury. This was no musical dilettantism: there was something threatening and even dangerous that rose up out of enormous depths, a kind of craving for movement; a mute prehistorical malaise was exuded by . . . the almost flagellant zeal of the guards in Mikhailovskii Square, and it whetted the Petersburg of that day (the year 1905 had not yet struck) like a knife. . . .

Hofmann and Kubelik . . . [held] sway over the stunned musical mob . . . [they] would try with all the means of their art . . . to chain and cool the unbridled Dionysian element. . . . But what in their performance was clear and sober served only to enrage and incite the crowd. . . . Such was the power in the rational and pure playing of those two virtuosos. (88–90; *SS,* 2:71–73)

Art is subtly charged with ever greater power as the turmoil and excitement of the intellectual commitment and ideological confusion experienced by the adolescent hero seeking to comprehend the age in its entirety are portrayed through both emotional responses to his environment and intellectual efforts to interpret history through aesthetic models:

I was troubled and anxious. All the agitation of the times communicated itself to me—from the longing for suicide to the expectation of the end of the world. The literature of problems and ignorant universal questions had just taken its gloomy malodorous leave, and the grimy, hairy hands of the traffickers in life and death were rendering the very words life and death repugnant . . . the dull polka from [Andreyev's] *Life of Man* . . . the symbol of vulgar tawdry symbolism, was picked out . . . on the piano . . . in every house. . . .

That was all the vilest scum when compared to the world of the Erfurt Program, the Communist Manifesto, and agrarian debates. . . . (108–9; *SS*, 2:98)

Contemporary literature, dominated by symbolism, is represented both in the false values and vulgarity attributed to Andreyev and in the magnificent but ultimately alien productions of Komissarzhevskaya's Dramatic Theater. While on the one hand, in Andreyev's representation, the problems of "life and death" were perceived as vulgarized, on the other, the refined beauty of *Hedda Gabler* could be appreciated. Nevertheless, in Mandelstam's view, the aesthetics of symbolism could not be altered even by the artistic devotion of a Komissarzhevskaya:

Unlike the Russian actors of that day—and also, perhaps, of the present day—Komissarzhevskaia possessed an inner sense of music; she raised and lowered her voice just as the breathing of the verbal sequence required. Her acting was three-quarters verbal and was accompanied by only the most essential, spare gestures. . . . I do not think that any perspectives for the future of the theatre were opened up here. That chamber drama came to us from little Norway. . . . The apothecary from Christiania [Ibsen] was able to lure terror into a professor's hen-house and to raise to the heights of tragedy the maliciously polite squabbling of Hedda and Brack. (111; *SS*, 2:100–101)

Although the objective consciousness of the autobiographical narrator intrudes in this passage, it merges with the hero's subjective vision. The sensitive adolescent is represented as having fully experienced the pre-Revolutionary age. His struggle for new values is reinforced. Hence, his review of Komissarzhevskaya and her theater actually provides a necessary dialogue with Andreyev's "vulgar, tawdry" symbolism. Komissarzhevskaya's acting is received positively because of its emphasis on "the word." Her repertory, however, is considered inappropriate to Russia's complex needs.

The tribute to Komissarzhevaskaya concludes the penultimate chapter of *Noise of Time*. Mandelstam's programmatic statement, which opens that chapter, is followed first by a strangely lyrical passage on "revolution," and then by the drama review. Revolution is perceived as natural, inevitable, and genuine—the antithesis of symbolism: "A revolution is itself life and death and cannot endure idle chatter about life and death in its presence. . . . Nature—revolution—is an eternal thirst, an inflammation . . . (110; *SS*, 2:99).

In this way, the period of "Adolescence" is associated directly with both the sociopolitical undercurrents of the day and with the search for a new and genuine aesthetic truth supporting an "attitude toward life," by rejecting the too refined as well as the vulgar tenets of symbolism.

Indeed, the young hero's efforts during this period to invoke aesthetic models to understand history and "life" lead him to equate Marxism (Kautsky) with Tyutchev:

Everything that represented an attitude toward life was greedily devoured. . . .

Early, O Erfurt Program, Marxist Propylaea . . . you gave a sense of life in those prehistoric years when thought hungered after unity and harmoniousness. . . . Is Kautsky Tiutchev? . . . But just imagine—for a person of a certain age and at a certain time Kautsky . . . is Tiutchev, that is, the source of cosmic joy, the bearer of a strong and harmonious attitude toward life, the thinking reed, a cover thrown over the abyss. (100–101; *SS*, 2:87)

Maturity and Conclusion

Nevertheless it is only in the concluding chapter of *Noise of Time*, when the poet-hero achieves "Adulthood" and merges with the autobiographical narrator, that he is finally mature enough to comprehend his "literary genesis" and write his autobiography. Only in this phase of "Adulthood," set in the post-Revolutionary period, when his aesthetic and historical consciousness have merged, can he identify himself as a "*raznochinets*-writer" and assimilate his past—the "Judaic chaos" of childhood, the "abyss" of adolescence—by confronting the challenge of the new age, the "wintry period of Russian history." In this phase, by identifying with the *"raznochinets*-writer," Mandelstam gains a new awareness of the bonds between art and history, between aesthetic and intellectual values, taking his aesthetic of "literary savagery" (*literaturnaia zlost'*) as his own autobiographical challenge. He thus confirms the power of art as a challenge to history and time, for the mature writer must judge the past by confronting it with the challenge of his own temporality and potentiality:

> Literary savagery! Were it not for you, what should I have to eat the salt of the earth with?
> You are the seasoning for the unleavened bread of understanding, you are the joyful consciousness of injustice, you are the conspiratorial salt which is transmitted with a malicious bow from decade to decade, in a cut-glass salt cellar, with a serving cloth! That is why I so love to extinguish the heat of literature with frost and barbed stars. Will it crunch like the crust of the snow? Will it brighten up in the frosty weather of the Nekrasovian street? If it is genuine, the answer is yes. (113; *SS*, 2:103)

How is this phase of "Maturity" actually conveyed in *Noise of Time?* First of all, it is established only in the final chapter, or epilogue, written in 1925, a year and a half after the completion of the major portion of the text. Here Mandelstam endeavors to present both an autonomous image of his narrator-hero as having achieved maturity as a *"raznochinets*-writer," and a synthetic portrait of his hero as having recovered his "literary genesis" by authoring his autobiography.

To represent this synthesis, Mandelstam first presents V. V. Gippius as a kind of alter ego to complement the image of the *"raznochinets*-writer"; his image is the *"raznochinets-litterateur."* By the way of explanation, Gippius had taught young Mandelstam "not literature, but the far more interesting science of literary savagery." He is symbolically recalled here as the "beast of literature" whose "lair of an apartment" once inspired young Mandelstam to imagine it as "literature's own house." In this final chapter of *Noise of Time,* Gippius emerges as Mandelstam's "companion."

Mandelstam's portrait of Gippius is thus presented both subjectively and objectively to express and explain the source of the autobiographer's self-image and his aesthetic of conscience: "literary savagery." The doctrine of "literary savagery," acquired by the adolescent schoolboy from his "teacher of literature," is here adopted by the mature poet-autobiographer as the aesthetic bond uniting protagonist and autobiographer.

The epilogue opens with a meeting of the two companions against the emblematic background of St. Petersburg's post-Revolutionary wintry night atmosphere. The imagery juxtaposes "cold" and "night," "heat" and "flame," "burning," "glowing," or "light" in the "winter of Russian history":

Towards *midnight* the waves of a *snowstorm* were *raging* along the streetcar tracks of Vasilievsky Island. . . . *Now,* the raspberry *globes* of pharmacies *burn there in the winter.*

My *companion* emerging from his *litterateur's lair* of an apartment . . . my *companion* became downright cheerful. . . . He bellowed for a cabby. . . . (112; *SS,* 2:102)

Further descriptions include: "The person who bellowed for a cabby was V. V. Gippius. . . . *He differed* from other *witnesses* of literature. . . . He had a kind of *feral relationship* to literature as if it were the *only source of* animal warmth. . . . I would come to him to wake up *the beast of literature.* . . . Never again was *literature to be a house, an apartment, a family . . .*" (114–16; *SS,* 2:104–6)

Finally, to support the complex of values presented in this concluding chapter, Mandelstam once again summons up a Pushkinian subtext, *Feast During the Plague,* which suggests a fuller understanding of the aesthetic of "literary savagery." Pushkin's "little tragedy" provides the model.

Besides echoing Pushkin's dramatic formulation of the theme of individual destiny, the subtext reinforces Mandelstam's idea that poetry's power arises out of attempts to "avert catastrophe," and affirms his idea that poetry is essential to the survival of humankind. Furthermore, while expressing the anxiety with which he, as a poet, faces the challenge of the future, it encourages the idea that literature is the "only source of warmth" in "this wintry period of Russian history."

Although there is no direct reference in *Noise of Time* to the "Hymn to the Plague" recited by Pushkin's hero, Walsingham, it emerges as a highly significant subtext, for the final chapter is bathed in images that mime its imagery, just as the poet's theme of faith in the survival of literature is seemingly inspired by the challenge of the hymn's thematic statement. The applicable stanzas (1, 2, and 6) of the "Hymn" read as follows:

> When fearlessly King Winter swoops
> Upon us with his hoary troops
> And brings against us in his ire

A mighty host of frost and snow,
Then we will gather at the fire
And feast with cups of wine aglow.

The way we meet the Winter's tide
So let us meet the Plague outside—
With light, with lights ablaze, and wine!
And so with laughter and with jest
Come dance and drink, with praise divine
To hail her majesty, Queen Pest!

And so, O Plague, we hail thy reign!
We laugh at graves, at death and pain.
We die no cowards in the night!
We drink, carefree! The baneful breath
Of dying beauty's our delight,—
Our daring in the face of Death![3]

This subtext is far more complex than it might appear initially. Not only does it underscore and universalize Mandelstam's theme of individual human destiny realized through "the word" as the vehicle of cultural continuity, but it associates the challenge of catastrophe (chaos, abyss, revolution) with the challenge of the plague. Like Pushkin before him, Mandelstam appears to perceive historical destiny as but another aesthetic challenge. However, in contrast to Pushkin, he also calls for a new aesthetic challenge to history. Thus for Mandelstam, the Revolution is just another one of the series of challenges he had to confront as he was growing up: "Judaic chaos," which ultimately stimulated his childish imagination; the "abyss" of adolescence and symbolism, which he imaginatively challenged through his synthesis of Kautsky and Tyutchev; and now the Revolution, the "wintry period of Russian history." On the other hand, "literary savagery," the aesthetic of conscience, the moral force behind Mandelstam's Acmeist aesthetic as redefined in "On the Nature of the Word," evokes a response as intellectually vital as it is aesthetically novel.

In this way, Mandelstam's aesthetic of the post-Revolutionary period both affirms the need for literature and confirms its survival as a natural process, as natural as animal instinct or the alternation of the seasons. Mandelstam recognizes that at this historical moment new literature must be formed by "winter and night," just as Pushkin sensed that his heroes had to create new songs and new challenges to avert the imminent catastrophe of the plague outside. Mandelstam's autobiography concludes with the passage: "And *in this wintry period of Russian history,* literature, taken at large, strikes me as something patrician, which puts me out of countenance. . . . No one is to blame in this and there is nothing to be ashamed of. A beast must not be ashamed of its furry hide. Night furred him. Winter clothed him. *Literature is a beast.* Its furriers are *night and winter*" (117; *SS,* 2:108)

Thus, in the last period Mandelstam treats in his autobiography, his new aesthetic of conscience, "literary savagery," is proffered as the successor to both the childishly naive "police esthetics" of the 1890s and the adolescent "esthetic of the intellect" marking the 1900s. Just as Nadson's poetry reading for the Literary Fund expressed the Russian intelligentsia's cultural zenith in the 1890s, and Komissarzhevskaya's *Hedda Gabler* reflected the culmination of cultural values in the 1900s, so Pushkin's *Feast During the Plague* conveys the post-Revolutionary "*raznochinets*-writer's" new aesthetic challenge.

Mandelstam's autobiography is thus reinforced by its literary symbolics, refracted through references to three key "performances," each of which culminates a phase in the poet's "literary genesis" and marks the juncture of the three parallel periods in Russia's cultural history treated in *Noise of Time.*[4]

The symbolics of Mandelstam's autobiography reinforce and develop the thematics of his text, and in particular the theme of the poet's destiny as the bard of Russia's cultural history, preserver of cultural continuity, indeed, as the bard of transition from the tranquillity of the nineteenth century to the challenge of the twentieth. Thus, through the art of his autobiographical act, Mandelstam articulates for the first time the tension between his life experience and its aesthetic interpretation.

Chapter Five
1921–1925

Death grows purer, misfortune saltier,
And the earth truer, and more fearsome.
> (no. 126, "I was washing at night," 1921)

For some, the salty imperatives of cruel stars
To be transferred to a smoke-filled hut.
. . . For some—the stern salt of solemn injuries.
> (no. 127, "For some, winter is arrack," 1922)

O life, fragile as clay! O dying age!
> (no. 140, "January 1, 1924," 1924)

The First Half of a Decade

The early 1920s, which witnessed Mandelstam's awakening interest in literary prose, also provided the impetus for *1921–1925,* the last collection of lyric poetry allowed to appear in print during the poet's lifetime. Both the prose and poetry of this period initiate a new direction in Mandelstam's poetics. *1921–1925,* together with versions of *Stone* and *Tristia,* was included in *Poems* (*Stikhotvoreniia*), the last collection of verse Mandelstam supervised. The publication of *Poems* in 1928, accompanied as it was by the appearance of a volume of his major literary prose subsumed under the title *Egyptian Stamp* (Egipetskaia marka), and a volume of essays, *On Poetry* (O poezii), unfortunately marked the peak of Mandelstam's career as a published poet. This "collected works" was made possible only through the personal intervention of his political patron, Bukharin.[1]

The early 1920s were one of Mandelstam's most prolific periods. The majority of poems in *1921–1925* emerged as part of an extraordinarily intense creative impulse spanning 1922–23, years that also witnessed his first efforts in literary prose, including *Noise of Time* and several shorter autobiographical, historical, and semifictional prose vignettes, such as "The Return," "Mensheviks in Georgia," "Batum," "The Fur Coat," and "The Grotesque," all autobiographical memoirs; "The Bloody Mystery Play of January 9," a dramatic historical commemoration; and the Moscow vignettes "Cold Summer" and "Sukharevka." In addition, he wrote numerous original essays including "On the Nature of the Word," "Badger Hole," "The Nineteenth Century," "Literary Moscow," "Literary Moscow: Birth of Plot," "A Letter about Russian Poetry," and "A Few Words about Georgian Art," all 1922; and "Notes on Poetry," "Storm and Stress," a published interview in *On Guard,* "Humanism and the Present," "Henri-Auguste Barbier," "The Moscow Art Theatre and the Word," and "An Army of Poets" in 1923. His seminal essay on prose, "End of the Novel," although first printed in 1928, may also have been conceived earlier, as part of his interest in prose forms. And last, but hardly insignificant for Mandelstam's life in the 1920s, 1923 also witnessed an intensification of his work as a translator.[2]

This period was also a time of vital aesthetic growth. Thematically, Mandelstam's central concerns with conscience, the moral perspective, and the challenge of earthly existence in the new Soviet age are evident in both his poetry and prose. Stylistically, he emphasizes the inner logic of association in his writing through greater reliance on syntactical, grammatical, and phonic connections to achieve textual coherence as opposed to objective narrative constructions based on the logic of semantic anticipation. What is more, his interest in prose forms seems to have coincided with his interest in the longer forms of lyric poetry, the meditative ode and elegy, genres popular in Russia at the end of the eighteenth and the early nineteenth centuries.

Although it contains a mere twenty poems, *1921–1925* includes several of the poet's lengthiest and most complex works, for example, no. 136, "Finder of a Horseshoe" ("Nashedshii-podkovu"), no. 137, "Slate Ode" (Grifel'naia oda"), and no. 140, "January 1, 1924."[3] *1921–1925* is primarily a collection of meditative poems initiating a new direction in which the authorial presence in the form of an autobiographical imperative mediates between the poet's contemplation of history and contemporary reality and his quest to fathom the relationship between the moral imperative and source of creative power. *1921–1925* serves as a major transition between the earlier and later poetry.

In both the poetry and prose of the 1920s we find a profoundly intensified emphasis on moral consciousness illuminated by his reformulation of Acmeism in "On the Nature of the Word" and reinforced through poetic reminiscences of the Russian meditative tradition.

Mandelstam's concern, however, was not with imitation or stylization, but with the reexamination and reinterpretation of the themes, forms, and values of the past in prose and verse genres appropriate to his unique twentieth-century vision.

Mandelstam's poetics of cultural continuity and his philosophical and psychological ambivalence toward the new social order depicted in *Tristia* are now combined with the intensity of the personal challenge to live in the new age and find some means of expressing allegiance to it. Simultaneously, however, he reaffirms his Acmeist prerogative to transfer to the new age the moral principles of humanism and, in particular, of the Russian eighteenth and nineteenth centuries despite real and potential sacrifice. The poet's covenant with the new age thus becomes a covenant of salt, of conscience, enunciated in several poems of this period—"to transfer the salty imperatives of cruel stars to a smoky hut"—and of "literary savagery," as evoked in *Noise of Time*:

Literary savagery! Were it not for you, what should I have to eat the salt of the earth with?

You are the seasoning of the unleavened bread of understanding, the joyful consciousness of injustice. . . .

The poems of *1921–1925* differ considerably from the lyrics of *Stone* and *Tristia* in theme, form, and semantic density. Their far more personal, meditative, and even metaphysical inspiration is evoked in the dominant themes of time, conscience, the poet, and the age. Their lyric hero is a far more self-conscious speaker, aware of the fragility of life and art, alternating between outbursts of fear and courage, a desire for human warmth and metaphysical yearning. Experimentation with structure and form, rhythm and rhetoric, and contrast and synthesis, as well as emphasis on motifs and images of contemporaneity, memory, history, conscience, illness, death, darkness, and winter, expand the breadth and depth of these poems, linking them closely with the literary prose that comprises such a significant part of Mandelstam's oeuvre in the 1920s and early 1930s.

On the other hand, while Mandelstam's poetry became more personal at this time, it also became more abstract and philosophical. Indeed, this period witnessed a thematic and stylistic synthesis of poignant lyricism with elevated moral inspiration, reminiscent of the Russian meditative tradition going back as far as Lomonosov and Derzhavin, and including Baratynsky, Pushkin, Tyutchev, Lermontov, Fet, and Annensky, and, among his contemporaries, Akhmatova. This tradition emerges again in the poetry of the 1930s.

The aesthetic lyricism of such *Tristia* poems as "I have forgotten the word" is intensified and personified, while the moral inspiration of earlier philosophically charged essays like "Peter Chaadaev" surfaces in both the prose and poetry of this period. What is more, just as "Word and Culture" served as a companion piece to *Tristia,* so do the ideas promulgated in the theoretical essays of 1922–23 illuminate the poems of *1921–1925.*

"I was washing at night in the courtyard"

"I was washing at night in the courtyard" (no. 126, "Umyvalsia noch'iu na dvore"), written in the autumn of 1921, is a lyric reformulation of Mandelstam's Acmeist principles in "On the Nature of the Word." It is possible that this poem, like "Concert at the Station" ("Kontsert na vokzale," no. 125) which opens this collection, is a concealed tribute to his dear friend Gumilev, whose execution on 25 August 1921 for alleged counterrevolutionary activities stunned the literary world. Mandelstam's new emphasis on the moral consciousness of humanism, the ideal of manliness or stoicism, and the sacred character of poetry certainly reflects the basic values of Gumilev's verse, both its man-centered thematics—indeed the ideal of masculine heroism dominating his earlier collections—and the metaphysical tendency of his later poetry:[4]

Acmeism is a social as well as a literary phenomenon in Russian history. With Acmeism a moral force was reborn in Russian poetry. . . . Until now the social inspiration of Russian poetry has reached no further than the idea of "citizen," but there is a loftier principle than "citizen," there is the concept of "Man."

As opposed to the civic poetry of the past, modern Russian poetry must educate not merely citizens, but "Men." The ideal of perfect manliness is provided by the style and practical demands of our age. . . . man must become harder, for he must be the hardest thing on earth; he must be to the earth what the diamond is to glass. The hieratic, that is, the sacred character of poetry arises out of the conviction that man is harder than anything else in the world. (*SS,* 2:258; *CPL,* 131–32)

Furthermore, the poet-persona's cognizance of real-life experience as "more fearsome" as well as simple and stern, pure and true, also reveals an important aspect of the poet's literary autobiography, in another possible reference to Gumilev's execution in the form of a dialogue with his former wife, Akhmatova, on the topic of the challenge of harsh reality as opposed to yearning for death. Ronen points out that the mood reflects Gumilev's "pensiveness of a friend" from his early poem, "The Magic Fiddle" ("Volshebnaya Skripka"): "And the dismal chill of death will swathe your body as if with a cloth, / And your bride will burst out sobbing, and your friend will grow pensive."[5] In his poem Mandelstam voices his acceptance of a new moral covenant as his challenge to death, time, and change.

In "I was washing at night in the courtyard" the poet announces his moral covenant as a new aesthetic principle, thus superseding the purely aesthetic pain of "I have forgotten the word. . . ." His covenant of salt, expressed here and in the poem's sequel, "For some, winter is arrack. . . ," corresponds to "literary savagery" in *Noise of Time*.

> I Was Washing at Night
>
> I was washing at night in the courtyard,—
> The firmament shone with coarse stars.
> A star-beam is like salt upon the axe,
> The barrel grows cold, its edges brimming over.
>
> The gates are fastened with a lock,
> And the earth's conscience is stern,—
> Purer than the truth of coarse linen cloth,
> Rarely found anywhere is the warp/foundation.
>
> Like salt, the star melts in the water barrel,
> And the water, now cold, grows blacker,
> Death grows purer, misfortune saltier,
> And the earth truer, and more fearsome.
>
> (no. 126, 1921)

The opening statement—which announces the fact that the speaker was washing in the courtyard at night—is misleading in its simplicity and immediacy, for in context this is an act of purification preceding the meditative act central to the poem's thematic focus and its final revelatory conclusion, the poet-speaker's own cosmic awareness.

In his role as participant in the simple ablutions of daily life, in his experience of the earthly world, and in his meditation on that experience, characterized as harsh, cold, and dark in the first stanza, the speaker comes to recognize the ultimate truth of being and accept its challenge.

The *realia* of the physical experience are cleverly juxtaposed to, and synthesized with, motifs and images of the metaphysical realm—night, cold, darkness, star, star-beam. On the level of ordinary daily life, the poet-speaker washes outside on a cold, dark night as the star-light strikes the icy water in the barrel. On the metaphysical level, he performs an act of purification under the watchful eyes of the firmament, preparing for cosmic revelation.

It is important here to understand how Mandelstam's lyrics operate simultaneously on the physical and metaphysical levels. The poet would attempt to describe this process a decade later in *Conversation about Dante,* the unique statement of his poetic credo, where he describes Dante as "a strategist of transmutation and hybridization" who worked in accordance with the "law of transmutable and convertible poetic material," an apt description of Mandelstam's own method. Consequently, we may note here how the external setting of this poem essentially catalyzes its action, which is internal and meditative. While in the first two lines of stanza 1 the act of washing suggests the hardships of an austere existence, the comparison of the star-beam shining on the ax to "salt" in the second half of the stanza suggests an undercurrent of anxiety that goes beyond ordinary life. Hence, in the first stanza both austerity and anxiety seem to define the speaker's mindset.

Subsequently, the courtyard as observed by the speaker impels him to evaluate his surroundings and to meditate upon his earthly existence. In stanza 2 his vision is rapidly elevated from the immediate physical surroundings—"The gates fastened with a lock"—to a metaphysical consideration of the relationship between the harsh demands of earthly life and its moral imperative—"the earth's conscience is stern." The solemn tonality of this line carries over into the last two lines, as he contemplates the purity and truth of "coarse linen cloth" with respect to the fundamental "warp" or "foundation" (*osnova*) of earthly existence. In context, *osnova* can mean both "warp" in connection with the linen cloth (or towel) and "foundation" with reference to the earth. Indeed, its placement in the final position of stanza 2 emphasizes it as an element unifying the poem's primary semantic levels—everyday life and metaphysical consciousness.

In the final stanza, the speaker's metaphysical awareness grows as his consciousness of the moral principles of purity and truth expands the meditation of stanza 2. The "foundation" or principle of life on this earth is more precisely defined, and the covenant of salt accepted:

"Death grows purer, misfortune saltier, / And the earth truer, and more fearsome." The integration of the concepts of purity and truth with misfortune and fear makes the poet-speaker's sense of cosmic understanding, indeed revelation, more poignant than anything expressed in Mandelstam's pre-1921 poetry.

Thus the poet's acceptance of life on this austere earth grows out of his gradual metaphysical awakening to the earth itself as the foundation of morality and truth. Once he had located the source of his moral principles, his sense of psychological freedom allows him to come to terms with his anxiety and to accept the covenant of salt. This concept of the earth as the source of truth continues as a central focus in Mandelstam's poetry of the 1930s.[6]

Stylistically, it is essential to recognize how Mandelstam's modernist techniques—what he termed the "transmutation and hybridization" of "transmutable and convertible poetic material"—are utilized both in his juxtaposition of lexical elements and in his "transmutation" of anticipated syntactical components so as to reinforce the poem's thematic and semantic structures.

First of all, as we have mentioned above, the first-person perspective dominates the entire first stanza and the opening line of stanza 2 as the speaker describes his surroundings in concrete terms. However, the second line of stanza 2—"And the earth's conscience is stern"—provides a transitional shift from concrete description to meditation, introduced by means of syntactical motivation, that is, through the use of the coordinate conjunction "And." Although logically and semantically the reader senses a shift in tonality, the syntax acts as if to retard the transition and continue the descriptive mode. Line 2 is actually a generalization that not only sums up the earlier physical and psychological description of setting, but prefigures the philosophical meditation to follow.

Similarly, syntactical motivation links the two distichs of the final stanza. The series of epithets in the comparative degree presented in the last distich—"purer," "saltier," "truer," and "more fearsome"—not only reiterate the epithet in a parallel position in the third line of the preceding stanza—"purer"—but are associated with the first distich—the list begun by "blacker."

Second, the association of abstract and concrete, of poetic and nonpoetic lexicon, corresponds to the bonding of the speaker's real, down-to-earth, psychological experience with his metaphysical meditation on the moral essence of earthly truth.

In stanza 1, the first and last lines contain only the lexicon of everyday life: "I was washing at night in the courtyard" and "The barrel grows cold, its edges brimming over." The two central lines, however, contain a "hybridization" of poeticisms—"firmament," "stars," "starbeam"—with obviously nonpoetic words—"coarse," "axe." This juxtaposition jars the reader's consciousness and prepares him for the extraordinary associations that follow.

For instance, the comparison of "star-beam" and "salt"—concrete words but with symbolic implications—is followed first by the personification of the earth, which has a "conscience." Second, by presenting such nouns as "earth" and "water" in the same series as "death" and "misfortune," Mandelstam affects an interchange of attributes, or a "transmutation" of the poetic material. "Earth" and "water" are not merely personified; they are "converted," acquiring tragic human qualities. "Death" and "misfortune," on the other hand, are concretized and brought closer to "earth" and earthly reality.

Thus the juxtaposition of the nouns and epithets that follow emphasize this mutual interchange of qualities, or the "transmutability and convertibility of [Mandelstam's] poetic material": concrete nouns are given abstract attributes, abstract nouns—concrete attributes. The intimate association and interchange of the abstract and concrete suggest that the relationships are convertible, and hence belong to a single semantic field. In this way, the speaker's growing awareness is simultaneously physiological, psychological, philological, philosophical, and cosmological. Indeed, the poem's conclusion is "transmuted" into a series of aphorisms, of truths that reinforce, reaffirm, and define the poet-speaker's newly revealed *osnova*—the moral foundation underlying the truth of contemporary life and its ultimate challenge of stern austerity, coarseness, and savagery.

Mandelstam's continuing dialogue with his cultural heritage also requires commentary here because of its prominence in his poetics. As we have seen in the earlier collections, dialogue is essential to Mandelstam's poetics of cultural continuity and reflects his Acmeist emphasis on cultural memory. In the 1930s, he speaks of "dialogue" or "conversation" as essential to his poetic credo in *Journey to Armenia* and *Conversation about Dante*.

Omry Ronen has shown that a "principal subtext" and perhaps a pretext for writing "I Was Washing at Night" is a poem by Anna Akhmatova entitled "Fear" ("Strakh").[7] It is worth citing it here to show how Mandelstam responds to its theme and imagery:

Fear, sorting things out in the darkness,
Aims a moonbeam straight upon the axe.
Behind the wall a rattle is heard, ominous,—
What is there: rats, a ghost, or a thief?

In the stuffy kitchen he splashes water,
Keeps account of rickety floorboards;
With a glistening black beard,
He would flash behind the garret window—

And calm down. How wicked and deft he is:
He has hidden the matches and blown out the candle.
It would be better [to face] the gleam of the muzzles
Of the rifles directed at my breast.

It would be better, in a green city square,
To lie down on an unpainted scaffold
And, to the cries of joy and groans,
To be drained dry of my red blood.

I press to my heart a smooth little cross:
God, restore peace to my soul.
A torpidly sweet smell of decay
Rises from the cool bed-sheet.

(trans. Ronen)

Akhmatova's theme reflects a generalized fear of life, time, and change. Awakened by a nightmare, fear is vividly personified and death agonizingly anticipated by the speaker. She subsequently yearns for death as a release from the agony of life. Mandelstam directly contrasts what he perceives as Akhmatova's unmanly yearning for death with Gumilev's expressed values of manliness, heroism, and the ultimate challenge of stern austerity, as reworked in his essay "On the Nature of the Word."

"For some, winter is arrack"

The following year Mandelstam wrote a sequel to "I was washing at night. . . ," entitled "For some, winter is arrack and blue-eyed punch" (no. 127, "Komu zima—arak i golubo-glazyi punch"), in which he associates his personal destiny as a man and as a poet with human destiny, and the moral, "salty imperatives of cruel stars." The poet-speaker perceives his role as "transferring the salty imperatives of the stars to the smoky hut" of a "fortune-teller," and hence seeking to divine the future, a motif reminiscent of "Tristia." However, this act demands terrible sacrifice. The purity of the earth ("the white, white snow") makes such demands on his conscience ("brings such pain to my eyes") that he experiences agony. The poem's poignant conclusion reads: "But the white, white snow brings such pain to my eyes."

For some, winter is arrack and blue-eyed punch,
For some, fragrant wine with cinnamon,
For some the salty imperatives of cruel stars
To be transferred to a smoke-filled hut.

Some warm chicken droppings
And witless warmth of sheep;
I'd give everything for life—I need care so much—
Even a kitchen match could make me warm.

Look: all I've got in my hands is an earthenware jug
And the stars' twittering tickles my weak ear,
But you can't help loving the yellow grass and earth's
Warmth through this wretched featherbed.

Softly stroking fur or rustling in the straw,
Starving like an appletree wrapped against winter,
Being drawn to someone senselessly and tenderly,
Or fumbling in the dark, and waiting patiently.

Let conspirators like a flock of sheep hurry
Through the snow, and let the snow crust squeak,
For some, winter is wormwood and bitter smoke—a nightlodging,
For some—the stern salt of solemn injuries.

If only I could hoist a lantern on a pole, and my dog
Running ahead, walk beneath the salt of the stars,
And with a jugged rooster call at the fortuneteller's hut,
But the white, white snow brings such pain to my eyes.

(no. 127, 1922)

The protagonist's acceptance of the covenant of salt[8] is represented four times in this poem. It appears first in stanza 1 as his moral destiny: "[to transfer] the salty imperatives of cruel stars . . . to a smoke-filled hut." Second, it emerges in stanza 3 as his poetic impulse, "the stars' twittering tickles my weak ear," and the metaphysical imperative penetrates the cozy warmth of the simple, earthly existence he so yearns to maintain (stanzas 2–3). Third, in stanza 4 it occurs as sacrifice: "the stern salt of solemn injuries." The implication here is that the covenant of salt involves not just the hardship of daily life, but the more bitter pain of "solemn injury," moral as well as physical pain. And finally, in the concluding stanza, the ultimate sacrifice demanded by the poet's acceptance of the covenant of salt is presented as a conflict between poetic imagination ("If only I could . . .") and harsh reality ("But the white, white snow . . .). In acknowledging that he too is merely an inhabitant of this earth and thus subject to its laws, he perceives that his quest to divine the future will only result in pain. His would-be idyllic vision—dog at his side, jugged rooster in hand, out seeking his fortune—must be sacrificed.

"On the Nature of the Word" attempts to define and concretize Mandelstam's vision of simple, earthly existence as an ideal: "an inner Hellenism, domestic Hellenism as it were . . . suitable to the spirit of the Russian language . . . an earthenware pot, oven tongs, a milk jug. . . . The warmth of the hearth experienced as something sacred; . . . humanizing and warming the surrounding world with the most delicate teleological warmth. . . . Hellenism is a system, in the Bergsonian sense . . . which man unfolds around himself, like a fan of phenomena freed of temporal dependence, subjected through the human 'I' to an inner connection" (*CPL,* 127–28; *SS,* 2:253–54).

This "inner Hellenism" may be read as "poetry" and "the human 'I'" as the poet. Mandelstam thus attempts to protect mankind from time, change, and catastrophe by subjecting the external world to the poet's imagination, by subjecting all external "phenomena . . . through the human 'I' to an inner connection." His covenant of salt is thereby "Hellenized" or "domesticated" and brought in touch with "the most delicate teleological warmth." The protagonist of no. 127, by bearing the "imperatives of the stars to the smoky hut" of the fortune-teller, thus views his act as one of purification—walking beneath the stars, eternal and imperative—but also as an act of sacrifice.

This poem, then, suggests that the poet's destiny is intimately linked with the earth's, and hence with time and change. The human condition, life on earth amid catastrophe and change, disaster and death, is elevated to the realm of metaphysical poetry—yearning for purifying self-sacrifice to be achieved through art.

The Age

In one of Mandelstam's best-known poems, "The Age" (no. 135, "Vek," 1923–36),[9] the theme of the poet's self-sacrifice for the preservation of cultural memory and the attainment of the ethical principles of Acmeism is joined with that of the tragic relationship between the poet and his epoch. "The Age" is envisioned at least in part as the poet's alter ego. Stanza 1 affirms the poet's role, his moral imperative, and his Acmeist aesthetic, for the poet-persona seems to view his own "blood" as "the builder," indeed, as the only thing that can "glue together" past and present—"the vertebrae of two centuries."

> My age, my monster, who shall dare
> To look into the pupils of your eyes
> And glue together with his own blood
> The vertebrae of two centuries?
> Blood the builder gushes forth
> From the throat of earthly things;
> A parasite only trembles
> On the threshold of new days.
>
> A creature, as long as it has enough life,
> Must carry its backbone erect,
> And a wave [of blood] plays
> With the invisible vertebrae.
> Like an infant's tender cartilege,
> The age of infantile earth,
> Once again like a sacrificial lamb
> The sinciput of life is offered up.
>
> In order to tear the age out of its bondage,
> In order to found a new world,
> The joints of nodular days
> Must be bound together with a flute.
> It's the age that rocks the wave
> With human anguish,
> While in the grass a viper breathes
> With the golden measure of the age.
>
> And once again the buds will swell,
> A sprout of green will burst forth,
> But your backbone is broken,
> My beautiful, pitiful age.

And with a senseless smile
You look backward, cruel and weak,
Like a beast, once supple,
At the tracks of your own paws.

[Blood the builder gushes forth
From the throat of earthly things
And like a burning fish, flails
The warm gravel of the seas to shore.
And from the lofty net of birds,
Off the blue soaking blocks and shards
Apathy streams, indifference pours
On that fatal wound of yours.]

                                        (no. 135, 1923–36)

The poem begins with the poet-speaker's address to the "age," here personified as a "beast" or "monster," and given the physical attributes of an animal: "pupils," "vertebrae," "a backbone," and "paws." He is also endowed with certain human traits—"pitiful," "beautiful," "senseless smile," "cruel and weak," "supple"—and even attributes associating the historical age with nature and organic growth—"joints of nodular days," "buds will swell," "sprout green." In addition, the "beautiful, pitiful age," or the "dying age" as it is known in Mandelstam's other poems of this period ("Finder of a Horseshoe," "January 1, 1924," and "No, never was I anyone's contemporary"), is also presented as having been denied its chance to grow old before it was "sacrificed like a lamb" in the inevitable onrush of history.

In stanza 1 the speaker suggests that to understand "the age," someone must dare "to look into the pupils of [its] eyes," for only by looking back and recognizing the past might it be possible to "glue together the vertebrae of two centuries." In *Noise of Time,* Mandelstam suggested that comprehension of the past, of nineteenth-century Russian culture, became possible only after the Revolution, that is, as a result of catastrophic change. This poem presents a similar idea: understanding is a consequence of breaking the backbone of the "beautiful, pitiful" age.

In stanza 3, a more optimistic possibility is envisioned, that poetic creation—"the flute," emblematic of lyric poetry—can liberate the age from its bondage and join it with the future in a "junction of nodular days." The idea of juncture refers back to stanza 1. However, it is suggested that "a new world" may be established joining "nodular days," that is, "new days" that may sprout from newly emerging "nodes." This image is developed in lines 1 and 2 of stanza 4: "And once again the buds will swell, / A sprout of green will burst forth." An organic image thus extends the image of "new days" concluding stanza 1.

If this juncture of days in stanza 3 can give birth to life, then it will be as a result of art or poetry. Indeed, stanza 3 suggests that the artist has a role in molding the "new world": "The joints of nodular days / Must be bound together with a flute." Poetry is represented both by "blood the builder" and "sacrificial blood," and by whatever inspires union. The poet's function, then, is to catalyze as well as to create unity, continuity, juncture. As we have seen in the earlier collections, the Acmeist mission was synthesis and thus maintenance of cultural continuity. Here again, poetry is invoked to meet the Acmeist challenge.

On the other hand, stanza 2 seems to echo the strong statement made in *Noise of Time* that the age, characterized as "the entire nineteenth century of Russian culture," was not only "shattered, finished, unrepeatable," but was something "which no one must repeat, which no one dares to repeat." Thus, if "a creature" (the age) has enough vitality, it can and must "carry its backbone erect," but in this case we know the backbone is broken. Furthermore, even though "a wave [of blood] may play with the invisible vertebrae," it could never restore the backbone, make it vital again, and so it had to be sacrificed before its time to make way for the new age. Indeed, the last four lines of stanza 3 echo the last two lines of stanza 1, offering not pity for the passing age, but the suggestion that it may have been responsible for its own premature fall. That is to say, it acted like a "parasite" and "trembled / On the threshold of new days" rather than take up the challenge of the new (stanza 1). It is also perceived as having been cruel, itself "rock[ing] the wave with human anguish," that is, it did not allow new values to alleviate the "human anguish" of the past, but rather permitted "a viper" to breathe "the golden measure of the age," even allowed the ascendancy of negative values and hence caused its own downfall. Indeed, it has been pointed out that a parallel syntactical construction using the instrumental case links lines 5 and 6 of stanza 3, "It's the age that rocks the wave / *With* human anguish," with lines 7 and 8, "While in the grass a viper breathes / *With* the golden measure of the age," suggesting a "close relationship between the age and the viper."[10]

Stanza 4, the concluding stanza of the original version, summarizes the poem's thematic content by suggesting that the "threshold of new days" (stanza 1) may come about: "And once again the buds will swell, / A sprout of green will burst forth." However, the poet's attitude toward the new is ambiguous. As in *Noise in Time,* the speaker, now at some distance from the past, looks back objectively but also sympathetically, seeing it as "beautiful and pitiful." Nevertheless, he recognizes that the fine qualities of the past will inevitably disappear along with the ugly and cruel. This poem, then, as another example of Mandelstam's attempt to grasp the new age and somehow to express allegiance to it, continues to reflect his ambivalence.

Stanza 5, which was added to the original four stanzas of "The Age" more than a decade later in 1936, seems to reiterate the position taken in the original last stanza, except that it is more pessimistic. It suggests that sympathy will be replaced by "apathy" and "indifference" toward the "fatal wound"—the broken vertebrae of the old age—and that no longer will anyone be around even to try to "glue the vertebrae together."

In the 1920s Mandelstam vacillated greatly in his evaluation of the nineteenth century, often echoing the ambivalent conclusion to *Noise of Time* that the nineteenth century was "shattered, finished, irretrievable," and yet deserved to be "hailed like settled weather." His views ranged from those expressed in his essay, "Nineteenth Century" ("Deviatnadtsatyi vek"), where he condemned it as an era of relativism, abstract methodology, moral vacuity, and Buddhist indifference, to the ideas presented in his poem no. 141, "No, never was I anyone's contemporary" (1924), perceiving it as an affirmation of Russia's immortal heritage. Thus the ambivalence of "The Age" is not surprising, for it expresses the poet's attempt to synthesize contradictory feelings and values—love and pity for the past, to which he has close emotional ties, and hope, fear, and self-sacrifice for the new age, to which his conscience bound him.

The lengthier, more experimental meditative poems of this period—"Finder of a Horseshoe" (1923), "Slate Ode" (1923), "January 1, 1924" (1924)—treat the same themes of the poet, the age, time, and conscience, but in more complex structures.[11] Thus, in *1921–1925,* although Mandelstam envisions the mission of poetry as binding the best of the old and the new, and reaffirms the poet's function as synthesizer, he cannot overcome his ambivalence and pessimism. Although this collection reflects his struggle to realize the human experience as a challenge to history and time, his poetics of cultural continuity could not outweigh his growing sense of the enormity of the sacrifice required to remain a poet of conscience. His pessimism regarding the fragility of life and art resulted in five years of unbroken poetic silence, lasting from 1925 to 30 October 1930, when the return of his poetic voice coincided with the realization of his journey to Armenia.

The second half of the 1920s was a period of extreme conflict for Mandelstam in his personal and professional life. Although the published volumes of 1928 represented the acme of his professional recognition, Mandelstam had essentially ceased writing lyric poetry three years earlier, concentrating instead on translations to earn a living and on the writing of literary and critical prose. It was during this period that he developed his ideas on the "novel." "End of the Novel" may be read as a companion piece to "Egyptian Stamp," written during the winter of 1927.

"Egyptian Stamp," one of the poet's most imaginative prose masterpieces, is his closest approach to fiction. This surreal, nightmare vision of the awkward, frustrating, and terrifying experience of the young writer vainly struggling to grasp the past as it vanished in the turmoil of the present by imagining himself in the shoes of his hero, Parnok, may be read on one level at least as a reflection of the poet's desperate state of mind in the mid-1920s. The narrator's fear of being identified with his hero is evoked in an anguished personal cry: "Lord! Don't make me like Parnok! Give me the strength to distinguish myself from him." This inclines us to see Mandelstam's second effort to tell the tale of the St. Petersburg poet's life as the response to a second autobiographical impulse. Only this time, instead of reminiscences of childhood, he concentrates on the fearsome prospects for the mature creative consciousness in an alien environment, asserting: "It is terrifying to think that our life is a tale without a plot or hero, made up out of desolation and glass, out of the feverish babble of constant digressions, out of the delirium of the Petersburg influenza."

This tale is thus told in "my dear prosaic delirium" by an author who ultimately rejoices in the aesthetic freedom and catharsis of the autobiographical act: "What a pleasure for the narrator to switch from the third person to the first!" In his attempt to tell Parnok's story, Mandelstam juxtaposes his own attitudes as a writer, his own feelings, responses, and values to those of his hero. Parnok's life becomes a kind of foil for identifying and rejecting various responses to life.

Furthermore, insofar as "Egyptian Stamp" represents the narrator's abortive attempt at writing a novel, this piece reflects Mandelstam's theoretical ideas in "End of the Novel." He claimed that the novel had no place in the twentieth-century canon because the structure and existence of that genre in the nineteenth century were based on the intimate relationship between the extratextual and textual functions of biography, which no longer exist:

> It is clear that when we entered the epoch of powerful social movements and organized mass actions, both the actions of the individual in history and the influence and power of the novel declined, for the generally accepted role of the individual in history serves as a monometer indicating the pressure of the social atmosphere. The measure of the novel is human biography. . . . The future development of the novel will be no less than the history of the atomization of biography as the form of personal existence, even more, we shall witness the catastrophic ruin of biography. (*CPL,* 199–200; *SS,* 2:267–69)

The would-be author of "Egyptian Stamp"[12] thus makes abortive attempts to write a nineteenth-century novel, a novel whose "measure" is "human biography." In the end, the third-person narrator expresses his relief at being able to switch from third person to first, for the "measure of the novel" as "human biography" is no longer sufficient: only subjective consciousness remains. In his subsequent works of literary prose—"Fourth Prose," *Journey to Armenia,* and *Conversation about Dante*—Mandelstam completely rejected the objective approach of the novel, or "biography," as inappropriate.

"Fourth Prose" had a cathartic effect on Mandelstam. According to his wife's memoirs, it helped to "release" him once again to write poetry. The two years during which he was embroiled in the Eulenspiegel Affair, she asserted, "were rewarded a hundred times over: the 'sick son of the age' now realized that he was in fact healthy. When he started writing poetry again, there was no longer a trace of the 'drying crust.' M's was henceforth the voice of an outsider who knew he was alone and prized his isolation. M had come of age and assumed the role of witness. His spirit was no longer troubled."[13]

If in "Egyptian Stamp," Mandelstam imagined himself in his humble hero's shoes experiencing the terrifying reality of a surreal nightmare, in "Fourth Prose" he imagined himself as Parnok's perverse antithesis. The protagonist of "Fourth Prose," although a social outcast, is cognizant of his rights as a poet and as a human being in an environment demanding his life. He triumphs over all forms of death and destruction, physical and psychological, individual and cultural, historical and political.

"Fourth Prose" is an extremely clever feuilleton attacking the Soviet literary establishment, a masterful polemic against "authorized" literature, and a diabolical exorcism of the "death trust," those who willed the destruction and defamation of "Mother Philology." Simultaneously, it is a glorious tribute to genuine truth in literature represented in citations to Gogol, Esenin, and Zoshchenko, and to faith in individual human action as expressed by his political patron Bukharin and his secretary. No less significant is the formidable attack on anti-Semitism, anti-intellectualism, and anti-individualism. Above all, however, "Fourth Prose" is the expression of an uncompromised and uncompromising poetic conscience that takes as its scourge truth, justice, morality, and irony embodied in the aesthetic ideal of "literary savagery" as defined in *Noise of Time.*

While *Noise of Time* poses the issue of the poet's challenge to society and history, "Fourth Prose" takes up that challenge and hurls it in the form of a prophetic curse against the forces of death and destruction, and specifically against the contemporary Soviet literary establishment. Indeed, in both its autobiographical and aesthetic structures "Fourth Prose" resorts to the thunder and all-consuming moral passion of Old Testament prophecy as well as the Mosaic Law, "Thou shall not kill," established in this work as a fundamental aesthetic precept. This piece confirms the aesthetic process in Mandelstam's poetics as a moral, intellectual, and cognitive act. The poet's renewed faith in himself and in the "creative spirit," following years of doubt and despair, seems to have resulted from an intensive personal revaluation of himself as a poet, as a man, and as a Jew. What is more, the instinctive moral and aesthetic response of the "*raznochinets*-writer" presented in *Noise of Time* as the ideal of "literary savagery" was finally realized in "Fourth Prose."[14]

Chapter Six
Journey to Armenia

I have cultivated in myself an "Ararat" sense . . .
I want to live in the imperative of the future passive
participle—in the "what ought to be."
(*Journey to Armenia*, 1931–33)

The Background

The recovery of Mandelstam's lyric voice is metaphorically revealed in
Journey to Armenia,[1] written in Moscow during the summer of 1931, a
year after his memorable "two hundred days in the Sabbath land." This
autobiographically engaged meditation joins the moral force of Old
Testament prophecy, enunciated so firmly in "Fourth Prose," to the
aesthetic force of contemplation, thereby providing a precious key to
the lyrics of the 1930s.

Journey to Armenia adheres to an "itinerary" shaped by the path Mandelstam followed in his quest for truth—"that truth which helps us to
form a better sense of ourselves in tradition"—and for a method to
articulate that truth—a "method of creative cognition, a suitable
means of gaining a sense of life." His "method of creative cognition"
mediates between the poet's contemplation of contemporary reality and
his meditation on the mystery of the creative impulse, whose origins
he seeks in the deepest structures of language and legend, whose eternal principles he ponders in the organic phenomena of nature, and
whose multiplicity of expression he experiences in the art, architecture,
and archaeology of Armenia. He came to perceive the land of the Covenant as the *cradle* as well as the *preserve* of language and culture.

Mandelstam's choice of an autobiographical mode emphasizes not
only the substance of what he contemplates, but the very process of his
interpretive creative experience, that is, how he intuits the mystery of
the creative impulse in the course of its revelation to him as his autobiographical imperative—his "obligation" to reassess his life and, after
five years of poetic silence, to renew and reaffirm his calling as a poet.

The duality of function implicit in Mandelstam's choice of genre is significant both in uncovering the complexity of his imperative and in formulating his poetics of self-knowledge through the intricate interweaving of moral-ideological and aesthetic-philological motifs. Indeed, a similar kind of autobiographical mediation distinguishes the lyrics of the 1930s from the earlier collections. Hence, the speaker of *Journey to Armenia* has much in common with the "lyric hero" of the *Moscow* and *Voronezh Notebooks.*

Armenia had long attracted Mandelstam. And for some time after his return, he continued to regard Armenia as symbolic of everything meaningful in human life: independence and happiness, human passion and hard work, human civilization, philology, and the source of "the Word," the geological and archaeological preserve of the eternal verities, and the font of "creative cognition," truth, wisdom, imagination, beauty. In addition, the images of Armenia and "the Armenian people" provided a standard against which to measure the human condition, and specifically on the moral-ideological level, life in Soviet Russia.

Mandelstam first envisioned Armenia as his "mythical Promised Land" in "Fourth Prose," where he imagines his journey in the conditional mood. In "Fourth Prose" the poet saw himself as he had once imagined the nineteenth-century Russian philosopher Chaadaev, who "took moral freedom as his holy staff and set off for Rome" "to fulfill a holy obligation." Mandelstam's "Jewish staff," which he saw himself carrying to Armenia—the "younger sister of the Jewish nation"—reflects that same imperative and "holy obligation." Only here it also symbolizes poetic freedom:[2]

I had a patron once, Mravian-Muravian, the People's Commissar of the Armenian nation, younger sister of the Jewish nation. He sent me a telegram. My patron died. . . .

I would have taken courage with me in my yellow straw basket piled high with fresh, clean-smelling linen, and my fur coat would have danced on a golden hook. And I would have descended at the Erevan station, bearing my winter coat in one hand, and my walking stick—my Jewish staff—in the other. (*SS*, 2:184–85; *CPL*, 317–18).

Journey to Armenia recalls ideological and philological motifs from "Peter Chaadaev" (1915) and "Word and Culture" (1921), essays explicitly concerned with the moral imperative in Russian culture, and "On the Nature of the Word" (1922), his Bergsonian defense of Acmeism as an aesthetic and moral vision.

In addition in viewing Chaadaev's experience as a paradigm of his own spiritual journey and subsequent return to Russia, Mandelstam noted Chaadaev's significance as a "personality" belonging "not to himself but to posterity," a highly significant statement for evaluating Mandelstam's poetry of the 1930s.

In "Word and Culture," Mandelstam posited the idea that the "imperative" was characteristic of "classical poetry," and, because it contained the "category of obligation"—that which "ought to be"—it must be the "prototype" of the poetry of the future:

> The silver trumpet of Catullus—*Ad clarus Asiae volemus urbes*—alarms and excites us more forcefully than any Futurist riddle. . . . I chose a Latin line because it is clearly perceived by the Russian reader as *a category of obligation*: the imperative rings more vividly in [Latin poetry]. Such an imperative characterizes all poetry that is Classical. Classical poetry is perceived as *that which ought to be,* not that which has already been. . . . Contemporary poetry . . . is naive. . . . Classical poetry is the poetry of revolution. (SS, 2:224–27; *CPL,* 114–16)

This idea is revived in the concluding chapter of *Journey to Armenia* where, in the name of "the Latin genius," Mandelstam assumes the function of his own imperative, what he calls the "Latin Gerundive" or the "verb on horseback," entering once more upon his self-appointed role as the bard of world culture. It is what Mandelstam refers to as the "Latin Gerundive," defined as the moral principle of "what ought to be" conjoined with the aesthetic principle of "what ought to be praised"—*laudatura est*—that which pleases us . . .'" which may be translated as his autobiographical and poetic imperative, as his moral and spiritual "obligation" to reassess his life and to renew and reaffirm his calling. Mandelstam's 1915 characterization of Chaadaev was prophetic of his own later role: "he seemed *to realize that his personality belonged not to himself but to posterity,* and thus he treated it with a certain humility: whatever he did, *he seemed to be* serving, *'fulfilling a holy obligation'"* (SS, 2:284; *CPL,* 83). In interpreting this realization as his imperative, Mandelstam made possible the extraordinary poetry of the 1930s.

The reader of *Journey to Armenia* must recognize that its "itinerary" is inspired by the poet's mythopoesis, for he experienced his pilgrimage to the land of the Covenant as his personal covenant. And, like Chaadaev before him, Mandelstam could feel secure in returning home, for Armenia would remain "in his breast." Nadezhda Mandelstam claimed this experience finally restored his "gift of poetry."[3]

By the time Mandelstam set off on his journey, his image of Armenia had been profoundly colored by his imagination and his reading. His knowledge of Armenian history, culture, and language derived as much from books as from personal observations. His reading of Persian and Armenian legends, of studies by Ivan Shopen, Nikolay Marr, and Josef Strzygowski, all gave credence to his mythopoetic vision of Armenia. While Shopen[4] went into great detail about the "phonetic ore" of the Armenian language, Marr's "Japhetic theory"[5] went even further, defining the Armenian language as mankind's original tongue. And the art historian Strzygowski[6] claimed that all Christian church architecture was derived from the Armenian "domed church on a square plan" with "niche buttresses."

Furthermore, in Mandelstam's mind Armenia was closely linked with the images of friends during that period of extreme social and political ostracism. Armenia was connected in particular with the young biologist Boris S. Kuzin,[7] who shared with Mandelstam an interest in Goethe on the one hand, and made efforts to establish analogies between the creative forces in art and nature on the other.

Structure and Themes

In terms of composition, *Journey to Armenia* consists of eight chapters of unequal length, resembling narrative prose fragments. Written in a style that creates the illusion of conversation or dialogue, the fragments are held together loosely through dialogic associations and recollected conversations with his primary interlocutor, Kuzin, and with himself.

The "itinerary" begins on the island of Sevan, where the poet defines his contemplative mood and conversational style: "I spent a month enjoying the lake waters . . . and *teaching myself to contemplate the two or three dozen tombs* scattered so as to resemble a flowerbed . . . [and conversing with the Armenian scholars gathered there]"[8] (*SS*, 2:137–143; *CPL*, 1:344).

The theme of contemplating life's continuum, omnipresent throughout this work, is almost immediately juxtaposed to the theme of learning to contemplate death and the theme of life's unpredictability as the ultimate challenge to death. The latter is joyously affirmed in the anecdote about the "corpse" who survived to the applause of his astonished audience: "That was the most beautiful applause I have ever heard in my life: a man was being congratulated for not being a corpse" (*SS*, 2:141–42; *CPL*, 1:348).

The theme of life's continuum, Mandelstam's poetic affirmation of life over death, is developed in the opening chapter in conjunction with the Bergsonian theme of intuition of the "élan vital" refracted through all the island's phenomena, natural and man-made. It is reinforced by the Christian theme of resurrection sustained by the imagery of Christian architectural monuments, and by the theme of cultural synchrony depicted in references to archaeological finds, art exhibitions, scientific, aesthetic, and linguistic theories, and, in particular, to discoveries of biological analogies linking creative processes in nature and in art. Last but not least, and of particular interest in assessing the later poetry, the theme of life's continuum emerges through concrete details depicting the simple, natural life of the Armenian people and its hold over the poet.

Throughout the journey, Mandelstam emphasizes the art of contemplation in discussions of works of art, in citations of Armenian legends, and in recollections of conversations about naturalists from Lamarck to Darwin to Kuzin and the circle of Armenian scholars Mandelstam encountered during his travels. Furthermore, the *realia* of the traveler's archaeological, linguistic, and biological observations are reconciled intuitively with the symbolic details of fantasy, myth, and legend. For example, the association of the poet's creative process with his keen perception of nature's organic process tends to give the outwardly fragmented form of the prose narrative a sense of unity of theme, technique, and aesthetic principle: "the very process of remembering crowned with the victory of memory's effort, is astonishingly similar to the phenomenon of growth." This recalls the poet's endeavor in "On the Nature of the Word" to synthesize the basic tenets of Acmeism— "the organic school of Russian poetry," viewed as inherently biological (intuitive) rather than legislative (based on canonized rules)—with a broader and more metaphysically oriented aesthetic vision.

The itinerary concludes in the "variegated terrain of wild and cultivated uplands, nomadic territories and vast pasturelands of Alagez," as the poet, while "riding horseback" and "conversing with myself," not only discovers, but *becomes,* his own imperative. This self-reflexive and self-transformational act, supplemented by the motifs of reprieve, renewal, and regeneration, seems to cause the philosophical, social, and ideological themes to burst through their aesthetic frame.

In each successive chapter Mandelstam expresses his growing fascination with Armenia and, above all, with the Armenian language, which the reader gradually recognizes as his metonymic representation of humankind and "the Word." In chapter 1, for instance, not only does the poet drink an imaginary toast "to the health of young Armenia," he also hails "its mighty language which we are unworthy of speaking. . . ." In chapter 2 he recalls his attempts to study Armenian and his attraction to "Japhetic books with their prickly script," going so far as to cite his "habit of regarding every Armenian as a philologist. . . ."

Furthermore, although Mandelstam's quest for the origins of language and the "nature of the Word" goes back at least a decade to his Bergsonian essay, it is in *Journey to Armenia* that he claims to have found in Marr's linguistic prehistory—his so-called "Japhetic theory"—a creative explanation for the "very deepest levels of language," indeed, the original language of mankind.

Along with charting his search for the origins of language and source of "the Word," Mandelstam intuitively outlined his quest for his own poetic imperative. The concluding lines of chapter 1 mention how "satisfying" and "instructive" he found it to immerse himself in the society of the Armenian people, a process that profoundly affected his sense of self and his entire value system, awakening him to the ultimate challenge of his imperative: to take cognizance of his own epoch "without fear" and to perceive in the Armenian people a "prototype" of the human condition: "The feeling for the fullness of life characteristic of the Armenian people, their coarse tenderness, their noble love of labor, their inexplicable aversion to anything metaphysical and their magnificent familiarity with the world of real things—all this kept repeating to me: now stay awake, don't fear your own age, don't be coy." (*SS,* 2:143; *CPL,* 349).

In the third chapter, a chance discovery of Paul Signac's manifesto *D'Eugène Delacroix au néoimpressionisme,*[9] affected Mandelstam "as if someone had summoned him by name" and transformed his life. This aesthetic imperative stimulated him to reexamine the process of learning to see. In keeping with the teachings of Delacroix and Signac, Mandelstam depicts his method of "penetrating a work of art." The entire fifth chapter, "Frenchmen," relates the art of contemplation to rules for the aesthetic contemplation of Impressionist painting. After passing through several stages in the process of "penetrating a work of art," including "calm self-confidence," "equilibrium" between observer and object, and the all-important process of "internalization," one reaches the final stage—"confronting the idea behind it."

According to Mandelstam, some mysterious and individual code must be intuitively grasped by the observer of a painting or reader of a text. Furthermore, upon leaving the impressionist exhibition, Mandelstam realized what a mysterious transformation he had undergone, "After the Frenchmen," he said, nature suddenly appeared anew, like something unnatural demanding aesthetic concretization: "the sunlight appeared like a phase of some waning eclipse, while the sun itself seemed to be wrapped up in silver foil."

Mandelstam's experience of his own aesthetic transformation focused his awareness on the power of art as an "obligatory" force. Indeed, in the preceding chapter he had linked the philological theme of language and the ideological theme of fear for the loss of cultural heritage with the idea of leaving behind "substantial proof of our existence"—the artist's obligation to posterity.

On Dialogue

Dialogue, as well as memory, eases the introduction of themes into *Journey to Armenia,* primarily through the recollection and re-creation of fragments of conversations. Mandelstam's dialogue with his primary interlocutor, Boris Kuzin, initiated in chapter 3 with reminiscences of parting, is concluded in chapter 7, the penultimate chapter, with the poet's "answer" to Kuzin's lengthy "eighteen-page letter." This dialogue creates an internal framing device to make credible the variety of themes included: the ideological theme, the juxtaposition of contemporary Soviet reality with the dream of "what ought to be"; the contrast of past and present in the attempt to make the poet's learning experiences relevant to universal truth; philological, philosophical, and psychological themes, including the joy of discoveries large and small, which need to be shared with a friend; ideas concerning the creative process in nature and in art, methods of "creative cognition," and the sources of language and legend.

In chapter 3, "Zamoskvorechie" (an area of Moscow), Mandelstam juxtaposes life in Moscow and Armenia. Longing to return to "the place where people's skulls are equally beautiful whether at work or in the grave," he complains bitterly about the "grim families of philistines living next door." Nevertheless, it was Zamoskvorechie that stimulated the fantasy of his "long-desired journey to Armenia," and later encouraged him to re-create his memories.

In chapter 7, "Ashtarak," Mandelstam no longer recalls the history of his friendship with Kuzin, nor reflects on their conversations in

Moscow or Erevan; neither does he comment on their mutual interest
in Goethe or in the relationship between the biological phenomenon
of growth and the creative process. Rather, he rejoices in his efforts to
convey to his friend personal responses, his acquisition of self-knowledge. He describes his emotional responses to Armenia, his "first sensual encounter with an Armenian church," his conscious cultivation of
his "sixth sense, his 'Ararat' sense," and he discloses his discovery of
wisdom in Armenian tales and legends. Most significant, perhaps, he
rejoices in his ineffable experience of the Armenian language:

> I experienced such joy in pronouncing sounds forbidden to Russian lips, mys-
> terious sounds, outcast sounds, and perhaps, at some deeper level, even
> shameful sounds.
> There was some magnificent boiling water in a tin teapot, and suddenly a
> pinch of marvelous black tea was tossed into it.
> That's how I felt about the Armenian language. (*SS,* 2:170; *CPL,* 372)

Mandelstam's quasi-dialogic structure is supported by his use of stylistic devices that include, most notably, an amalgamation of fragments, citations, tenses, and a "sliding" movement from topic to topic,
presented in chapter 3 in his description of the conversation at Kuzin's
farewell party:[10] "The subject of the conversation kept merrily sliding
about like a ring passed around the back, and the knights' gambit,
ever to the side, reigned over the table talk . . ." (*SS,* 2:149; *CPL,*
354).

In his presentation of Kuzin's biography and in his description of
the farewell party, the variety of subjects and the use of various tenses
cloud the reader's perception of Mandelstam's temporal and spatial
sense. Physically, he is in Moscow; mentally, he seems to be in Armenia. He alludes to being together with Kuzin in Moscow and in
Armenia; his thoughts and dreams of joining Kuzin once more in Erevan collide and merge with recollections of times spent together in
Armenia. The poet's "voice" thus takes on greater significance than the
actual time and space of his journey.[11]

The "conversation . . . merrily sliding about . . ." becomes para-
digmatic of the poetics of *Journey to Armenia* as a whole, for this seemingly discontinuous conversational style structures the introduction of
its various subjects, moods, and emotions; shapes moments of poetic
insight, reflection, and aphoristic judgments; and admits philosophical
and philological propositions and observations that might arise in in-
telligent conversation or in notes recorded in a journal.[12]

Furthermore, Mandelstam specifically emphasizes the value of "intimate conversation" over more formal methods of learning. His itinerary, then, may also be charted in terms of its numerous dialogues with the people he encountered, with the books he read, and with himself. The poet's quest is indeed best answered by "the warm light of oral instruction, the lucid didacticism of intimate conversation, [which] is far superior to the instructive and homiletic function of books."

In chapter 1 of *Journey to Armenia,* the quality of his conversations with the Armenian scholars on Sevan is described thus: "I preferred their peaceful company and the quality of strong coffee permeating their talk to the flat conversations of the young people, which as everywhere else in the world, revolved around examinations and physical culture" (*SS,* 2:140; *CPL,* 346).

In chapter 2, his conversation at the Institute for Oriental Peoples so impressed him that he contemplated semantic meaning at the "deepest levels of language." And chapter 3, arranged almost in its entirety as a dialogue, concludes with a direct address to Kuzin in the form of "belated reflections." The latter may be read as fragments of a letter to which chapter 7—the "answer" to Kuzin's "eighteen-page letter"—corresponds structurally.

Mandelstam's efforts to create the quasi-dialogic structure of *Journey to Armenia* are also of interest in prefiguring his last known manuscript, *Conversation about Dante,* a "conversation" rather than a "treatise" on his poetics.

One of the most significant subjects in the dialogue with Kuzin is the connection between scientific (especially biological) and aesthetic theories of the creative process, which extends the discussion found in "On the Nature of the Word." In chapter 3 of *Journey to Armenia,* the poet's "reflections" present his discovery of an unsuspected correlation between the organic "phenomenon of growth" and memory:

Without suspecting it, we are all carriers of an enormous embryological experiment: indeed, the very process of remembering, crowned with the victory of memory's effort, is astonishingly similar to the phenomenon of growth. In both instances, there is a sprout, an embryo, either some facial feature or character trait, a half-sound, a name ending, something labial or palatal, some sweet pea on the tongue, which does not develop out of itself, but only responds to an invitation, only stretches forth, justifying our expectation. (*SS,* 2:155; *CPL,* 359)

This discovery—which includes the idea that the environment is a force that "invites" the organism to grow and not something that pre-determines its "development"—also echoes "On the Nature of the Word" in affirming Mandelstam's ideological hostility toward contemporary theories of environmental determinism.

In opposing the theory of "invitation" to contemporary theories of "development," Mandelstam's neo-Lamarckian position (echoing Kuzin's) must be understood in terms of his ideological stance. In his view, deterministic theories could only limit men's vision:

No one, not even an inveterate mechanist, views the growth of an organism as resulting from the variability of the external environment. That would be far too presumptuous a conclusion. The environment merely invites an organism to grow.

Thus, for the environment, the organism is probability, desire, and expectation, while for the organism, the environment is a force which invites: not so much a covering as a challenge.[13] (SS, 2:164; CPL, 367)

Hence Mandelstam's concern with the fundamentals of knowledge or truth. While recognizing the potential of scientific research on the life processes, he seems to discount the possibility of discovering empirically the basis of the growth process, preferring Bergsonian "intuition." According to Mandelstam, "A plant . . . is the envoy of a living storm permanently raging in the universe, akin in equal measure to stone and lightning! A plant in the world is an event, a happening, an arrow, hardly some boring, bearded 'development'!" (SS, 2:154; CPL, 358).

This passage suggests a theory of immanence. The idea that "a plant in the world is an event" implies that its essence equals the fact of its existence, the very phenomenon of its creation. This simply cannot be explained in terms of contemporary theories predicting the cause and course of development.

The question of the appropriate "method of creative cognition" arises in chapter 6 in a tentative revaluation of Darwin, whose "geniality" charmed Mandelstam. However, the poet was forced to wonder at his own response: "But is geniality a method of creative cognition, a suitable means of gaining a sense of life?"

The relationship between intuition and deductive reasoning raised in his conversations with the natural scientists first emerges in chapter 2 in connection with his efforts to penetrate the "deepest levels of language," to seek out the origin of concepts: "At the deepest levels of language, there were not concepts, just directions, fears and longings, needs and apprehensions. . . ."

Mandelstam's method of "creative cognition" also supplements intuition by examining things anew, from an extraordinary perspective, in an unprecedented, unpredictable manner. For example, impressed by Lamarck's description of a strange butterfly, he wished to reexamine the entire world through its eyes: "suddenly I caught myself madly wishing to look at nature through the painted eyes of that monster." Hence, his interest in such "forbidden themes" as the physiology of reading . . . a rich, inexhaustible, and seemingly forbidden theme . . .," or his joy at "pronouncing sounds forbidden to Russian lips. . . ."

According to Mandelstam's theory of "creative cognition," the unpredictable, the perverse, the forbidden, the mysterious, even the whimsical, emerge as fundamental aesthetic elements. "Creative cognition" is thus a method using the most unconventional means to interpret and convey the mysterious, the inexplicable, the ineffable, including intuitive responses to a "summons," the "sixth sense," and "imperatives." In the final two chapters of *Journey to Armenia,* Mandelstam depicts his "attraction" or "propulsion" (*tiaga*) toward the Armenian language as the result of cultivating a "sixth sense in myself, an Ararat sense; I can feel the mountain's propelling force."

Mandelstam's journey, then, is basically a contemplative process; his quest—a search for some underlying, unifying creative impulse. Looking beyond and beneath the empirical, scientific data of contemporary Soviet theories of "development," he turned to the cradle of civilization, to the very "deepest levels" of language, to legend, poetry, and "the Word."

On Style

The style of *Journey to Armenia* reinforces Mandelstam's thesis, for his imagery frequently elicits bonds, comparisons, and conjunctions that the ordinary mind perceives as incompatible and incomparable. Mere contiguity, in accord with "creative cognition," is enough to establish associations such as the "physiology of reading" as an act of self-reflexive taxonomy: "When we are completely immersed in the activity of reading, we admire above all our generic attributes . . . we experience, as it were, the ecstasy of classifying ourselves in various ages and stages" (*SS,* 2:163; *CPL,* 366).

Similarly, in chapter 7, the linguistic apologue of chapter 2—the lesson of the "Japhetic novella"—is metamorphosed, as it were, into the formula of fairy-tale endings, into the legendary wisdom of the ages. The poet's "Japhetic novella" reads:

"Head" in Armenian is *glukh'e.* . . . . It contains the same root as the Russian word for "head." . . . But would you like a Japhetic novella? If you please: "To see," "to hear," "to understand"—all these meanings coalesced at once into a single semantic bundle. At the very deepest levels of language there were no concepts, just directions, fears and longings, needs and apprehensions. The concept of "head" was sculpted over a dozen millennia out of a bundle of foggy notions, and its symbol became "deafness"—*glukhota.* (*SS,* 2:144; *CPL,* 350)

In chapter 7, by recalling and expanding upon his "Japhetic novella," Mandelstam provides a creative variant on the conventional fairy-tale ending. The traditional ending reads: "Three apples fell from the sky: one to the storyteller, one to me, and one to the person who entertained you."[14] Mandelstam's variant, instead of focusing on the reward, emphasizes the relationship of legend to the formation of semantic concepts in language—seeing and telling, hearing and listening, and finally, understanding: "Three apples fell from the skies: the first for the one who told the tale [saw something and related it], the second for the one who listened, and the third for the one who understood. So end most Armenian fairytales" (*SS,* 2:171; *CPL,* 373–74).

Thus, according to Mandelstam's theory, just as prehistoric sounds coalesced "at some time in the past" into semantic meanings or concepts, so in time those concepts were effectively woven into the fabric of tale and legend, the repository of mankind's creative wisdom. Mandelstam thus gradually traces the continuum of "creative cognition," its sources and processes. He discovers and recovers the creative impulse, "the Word," everywhere: in architectural and archaeological finds, in the creative spirit of his dialogues with scholars and friends, in his experiences in the fine arts museum, in all aspects of his Armenian itinerary. Nevertheless, his happiest discoveries are expressed in joyous revelations of the origins of language and legends, and consequently in acknowledging his own "sixth sense" and recognizing his autobiographical imperative.

Recovery of his Poetic Obligation

In the final two chapters, Mandelstam's quest for the "truth which helps us form a better sense of ourselves in tradition" is finally realized. He applies his method of "creative cognition" as he articulates his mysterious, inexplicable experiences, cultivates his "sixth sense . . . an Ararat sense,"[15] and apprehends the mountain's "propelling force," now revealed as his protection against fate: "Now, no matter where fate may lead me, it already has a speculative existence, and will accompany me forever."

In the concluding chapter, Mandelstam's self-reflexive dialogue reiterates the joyous excitement conveyed in the preceding chapter in his correspondence with Kuzin. Fascination with language, indeed with philological reality, takes over as the poet asks himself which "tense," as opposed to which "epoch," he would "choose to live in." His emphatic answer, which invokes both choice and volition, merges the ideological theme of free choice with the philological theme: "I want to live in the imperative of the future passive participle—in the 'what ought to be.'" Philological reality—here expressed as the poet's medium and the mediating factor in his poetics—gradually associates the poet with his own medium and ultimately transforms him into his "glorious Latin 'Gerundive' . . . a verb on horseback":

(1) What tense would you chose to live in?

(2) "I want to live in the imperative of the future passive participle—in the 'what ought to be.'"

(3) I like to breathe that way. That's what I like. It suggests a kind of mounted, bandit-like, equestrian honor. That's why I like the glorious Latin "Gerundive"—it's a verb on horseback.

(4) Yes, the Latin genius, when it was young and greedy, created that form of the imperative verbal propulsion as the prototype of our entire culture, and not only "that which ought to be" but "that which ought to be praised"—*laudatura est*—that which pleases. . . .

(5) Such was the dialogue I carried on with myself as I rode horseback through the variegated terrain of wild and cultivated uplands, nomadic territories, and vast pasturelands of Alagez.

(6) In Erevan, Alagez was forever greeting me: "hello." . . .

(7) And I was propelled toward it, over the mulberry trees and the earthen rooftops.

(8) A piece of Alagez lived right there with me in the hotel . . . glassy black volcanic rock known as "obsidian."

(9) The approaches to Alagez are not fatiguing, and it is no trouble at all to reach the top on horseback. (*SS*, 2:172–73; *CPL*, 374–75)

The emphatic answer (2), "I want to live . . . ," is followed by (3), an explanation of the choice and an explication of his desire—"I like to. . . . That's why. . . ." The relatively static concept of tense presented in (1), the initial question, is thus transformed into (3), the active verbal form, the "Latin Gerundive," the "verb on horseback." Simultaneously, the excited, intense staccato voice hurrying to explain and defend his "answer" supplements the theme of choice represented by the verb "to want" (*khotet'*), with the more sensual theme of pleasure expressed in the repetition of the verb "to like" (*nravit'sia*).

The three themes of tense, choice, and pleasure are united here: choice is both a major ideological and aesthetic theme in this work; the tense chosen has ideological as well as philological implications; and the sensual theme, evoked in the intonation itself, is associated with tense and choice.

In (4), which opens with an emphatic "yes," the incipient themes all merge into the theme of the poet's function. Inspired by the revelation of the equivalence of the aesthetic function and ideological obligation, the poet is carried away—literally and figuratively—by "pleasure." The ideological and the aesthetic—"what ought to be" and "what ought to be praised"—are thus perceived as interrelated through their common origin in "the Latin genius" which "created that form of imperative verbal propulsion as the prototype of our entire culture."

The slightly archaic narrative style of (5) serves to clarify the linguistic metaphor of the "Latin Gerundive" and to bring both poet and reader back to earth at least momentarily, while retarding the reader with its striking subordinate clause, as if to ready him for the next major metaphorical leap to Alagez, which focuses the controlling image of this section (6–9). The explanation, however, suggests the poet's own metamorphosis into the "glorious Latin Gerundive"—the "verb on horseback"; the "dialogue," after all, is described as taking place while the poet literally "rode horseback" in the Alagez range (5, 9).

While the "propulsion" (*tiaga*) of the Armenian language and the poet's "sixth sense . . . [his] 'Ararat sense'[15] . . . the mountain's propelling force" ("chuvstvo pritiazheniia goroi") are invoked in the poet's dialogue with Kuzin in the penultimate chapter, this "propulsion" metaphor becomes the "imperative verbal propulsion" ("povelitel'naia glagol'naia tiaga") of the "Latin Gerundive" in the final chapter, where the poet experiences the feeling of being "propelled toward" (*tianulsia*) Alagez.

The reader, having encountered the suggestion of Mandelstam's own transposition into his medium, into the "verb on horseback" ("glagol na kone") can now recognize the metaphor linking the elemental linguistic power of the Armenian language (or "the Word") with the "Latin Gerundive" and "propulsion" (images of his imperative) toward the mountain, Alagez. The cumulative effect of these images heightens the poet's renewed sense of his "calling." His intuitive response to his imperative thus becomes synonymous with his method of "creative cognition."

The poet's *desire* to "imitate his medium—to live in the "imperative of the future passive participle," the "Latin Gerundive," to become a "verb on horseback"—is thus transposed into the poet's *act* of *imitatio*: he becomes the "Latin Gerundive" as he "rides horseback," propelled toward Alagez (5–9).

What is more, the imperative of the last line of the final paragraph of *Journey to Armenia* seems to confirm the "fact" of the transposition and affirm his status: "Last thought: *I must ride* around some other ridge" (*SS*, 2:176; *CPL*, 8:378).

This confirmation further identifies the poet with the "prototype of our entire culture, not only 'that which ought to be' but 'that which ought to be praised'—*laudatura est*—that which pleases us." Only as the bearer of culture through the ages can Mandelstam assume once again his poet's function. Thus the realization of his would-be journey returned to the poet his "gift of poetry"; and the highly poetic prose narrative *Journey to Armenia* traces in the poet's own words the creative process involved in his seeking to renew and reaffirm his calling. Mandelstam's "last thought" *is* his imperative acknowledged, the poet's own demand on himself to fulfill his function.

One question remains: how does Mandelstam's imperative unite the moral-ideological theme with the aesthetic-philological themes and images in this work? And why does the poet insert seventeen sparse paragraphs of the Arshak-Shapukh legend[16] immediately before his "last thought"?

It seems that it is only in this concluding section that the reader is brought to a full realization that the poet's moral-ideological obligation is no less significant than his aesthetic-philological imperative. The legend must be read in context. Its placement is structurally significant.

The journey having drawn to a close, the narrator chose a place to settle down for the night. Peace reigned, only to be shattered by the seeming intrusion of the legend.[17] The reader is subtly prepared for the legend only by the conversational style of the narrative, which allows for the insertion of varied topics; by thematic links subtly provided in the dialogue, mainly concerning ideological choice and poetic freedom; by the reference to "palace" in the line immediately preceding the legend: "I felt as shy as if I were in a palace"; and—most significantly— by free association with the inherent wisdom of the "typical ending" of Armenian tales mentioned at the conclusion of the penultimate chapter—will the "apple" be caught by the one who understands?

The legend concerns King Arshak, who was overthrown by Shapukh and banished to the fortress of Anioush.[18] Arshak was, nevertheless, granted a reprieve, the gift of a faithful servant. In the original legend, Arshak's former servant, the faithful Trasdamad, having saved Shapukh's life, was granted one wish. He used it to request a visit to Anioush to bring his former master, Arshak, back to life for one more day. When his "ticklish request" was granted, he regaled Arshak with a feast and then relieved him of his misery by killing them both.

In rewriting this legend, Mandelstam only partially accepts the paradigm. He emphasizes reprieve by omitting the fatal ending, but concludes his version far more ambiguously, with the servant's wish to grant his former master a reprieve: "one more day in full possession of his senses—hearing, tasting, and smelling—as he once was, when he found his greatest pleasure in hunting and planting trees." Mandelstam's version returns the reader to chapter 1, reintroducing the theme of life's continuum and the theme of the unpredictability of life as the ultimate challenge to death.

The legend has obvious autobiographical implications. Arshak's condemnation to the fortress of "unpersons" and his gift from a loyal friend parallel Mandelstam's own status—ostracism from the world of the literary establishment—and his reprieve—the gift of his loyal friend and patron, Bukharin, who offered him the journey to his "mythical Promised Land" as "one more chance" to be in "full possession of his senses."

The placement of the legend forces the reader to connect it with the poet's life, for, structurally, Mandelstam's text presents the story of a man who has not yet completed his journey. The absence of a finite ending underlines its autobiographical essence. Meaning is associated with the life that has been recollected, but even more with the auto-biographical imperative—the "Latin Gerundive" or "verb on horse-back"—behind the life *as yet* to be lived. Thus Mandelstam reasserted his will to live and confirmed his obligation to return to his calling: "*I must ride* around another ridge." The sinister implications of the subtext nevertheless remain just below the surface.

Mandelstam's creative reconstruction of the frightful tale of King Arshak into a legend reflecting, however ambiguously, reprieve, continuity, and faith in "creative cognition," prefigures the poetry of the 1930s, and specifically certain verses written in his Voronezh exile which echo his imperative:

> I must live, although I've twice died. . . .
> (no. 305, 1935)

> I must live, breathing and bolshevizing,
> And growing beautiful before death,
> Continue to visit and to engage people.
> (no. 312, May–June 1935)

> You—throaty Urals, broad-shouldered Volga
> Or this even steppe—behold all my rights—
> With a full chest I must continue to inhale them.
> (no. 366, 8 February 1937)

Chapter Seven

Moscow Notebooks

It's time you knew I'm also a contemporary,
I'm a man with a *Moskvoshveiia* label . . .
(no. 260, "Midnight in Moscow," 1931)

Any process involving the creation of form in
poetry presupposes lines, periods or cycles of
sound forms, as is the case with individually
enunciated semantic units.
(*Conversation about Dante,* 1933)

"How much we have to fear"

While *Journey to Armenia* is a conscious meditation on the return of
Mandelstam's lyric voice, the specific occasion marking that return was
Nadezhda Yakovlevna's nameday, celebrated in Tbilisi's famous Hotel
Oriant on 30 October 1930. The event is significant both as a source
of the poet's intimate lyric, no. 202, "How much we have to fear, you
and I" ("Kuda kak strashno nam s toboi"),[1] and as a sign of further
changes in Mandelstam's mythopoesis and poetic credo.

The primary motifs of this bittersweet lyric—fear, love, and the
relationship between experience and the imagination—not only suggest a realistic and frightening worldview, but introduce a common
human element into the autobiographical image of the poet-persona of
the 1930s that was barely present in the collection, *1921–1925.* The
sentient voice of the eyewitness and the lucid image of the man of his
generation support the presentation of common human morality as an
aesthetic impulse informing the later poetry. Mandelstam's poetic
credo is no longer dependent on cultural tradition and literary models,
for he has finally accepted the credentials of his historical self as integral to the image of his persona.

Nevertheless, Mandelstam's autobiographical persona must not be
confused with unmediated biography. Rather, his use of the autobiographical mode establishes the foundation for his new mythopoesis.

His myth of the poet as mediator reflects the "modernist" attributes of
his poetic consciousness described by Geoffrey Hartman as the "unmediated vision" in his book of the same title. Hartman's definition of
"modern poets" clearly applies to Mandelstam's work of the 1930s:

> The modern poet has committed himself to the task of understanding ex-
> perience in its immediacy. He has neglected the armature of the priest . . .
> and often, the inculcated respect for literary models. But therefore he comes
> to know the need of mediation only the more strongly. . . . [Having] lost the
> full understanding of revealed religion, [he] accepted the individual quest for
> truth and forced by this same quest to seek mediation, sought it neither in
> Christ nor in tradition but in the very things that caused [him] to seek: per-
> sonal experience and sense experience. . . . It is the artist who, acknowledged
> or not, pretends to the role of mediator. . . .
> Personal experience becomes the sole authority and source of conviction,
> and the poet a new intermediary . . . The modern poet is the Experimenter
> and, not rarely, the Self-Tormentor. His real mediation is to accept and live
> the lack of mediation.[2]

Indeed, Mandelstam's effort to recover a "sense of time" that so dominated *Noise of Time* and the verse of *1921–1925* gives way in the 1930s
to a literal and spiritual quest for a "sense of place." His painful search
for living space, not only in Leningrad, but in Moscow and then in
exile, may partially explain the impulse behind his psychological need
to find a "place" in Soviet life and his metaphysical desire to conquer
"space." His poet-persona's quest is enacted first in the earth and sky
of the "Armenian Cycle" and "The Octets," and subsequently in the
ultimate challenge of death expressed in the *Voronezh Notebooks* from the
"Black earth" cycle to "Verses on the Unknown Soldier."

In contrast to *1921–1925*, in which ambivalence and uncertainty
alternate with stoicism and conscience in the poet's contemplation of
the harsh new world, and where, fearing the loss of cultural memory
and seeking mediation in the form of divination, he ultimately despairs
of a resolution, Mandelstam's new mythopoesis gradually generates an
existential awareness of his function as "a new intermediary." The autobiographical mode of the 1930s not only reaffirms his renewed sense
of "rightness" as a lyric poet, but supplements his persona's image with
the values and perspective of a humble inhabitant of the contemporary
world, whose elemental love of life, sense of humor, and desire to define his place in the common destiny of his age, justify his role as poet-
witness.

Mandelstam's poetry of the 1930s is not mere civic poetry, however, for it elevates the speaker's everyday experience to the level of extraordinary aesthetic experience. Thematically, the common human experience is realized through the contemplation of the human condition; through fantasy, imagination, incantation, and exorcism; through emblematic images of cultural tradition and subtextual reminiscences of Mandelstam's own earlier work and other literary models. Structurally, his new poetics exhibit increasingly complex prosody, intricate phonosemantic devices, a new tonality derived to a great extent from clever use of dialogue and irony, and emphasis on the fluid process of poetry as continuous creation or "performance."

What is more, Mandelstam's new direction, initiated thematically as early as 1921 in "I was washing outside in the courtyard," now determines the reformulation of his poetic credo. Although partially enunciated in "Fourth Prose," *Journey to Armenia,* and in such lyrics as "How much we have to fear," it is not fully elaborated until 1933, in *Conversation about Dante* and in his subsequent lyrical cycle "The Octets."

The fact that a brief and novel love lyric (no. 202, "How much we have to fear, you and I" [Kuda kak strashno nam s toboi"]) opens the *Moscow Notebooks* is very significant. Written in response to the same impulse of renewed faith in the "Word" and the imagination as the "Armenian cycle," it contains a model for Mandelstam's motif of the poetic imagination as a shield protecting the poet, as it were, against time and contemporaneity.

While the playful yet bittersweet tone of this poem may also reflect Mandelstam's realization that his Armenian reprieve was drawing to a close and that he would soon be returning to the world of Soviet Russia with all its uncertainty and hostility, the speaker's negative perception of reality is nevertheless countered by his vibrant colloquial dialogue, sense of humor, and love of life, and by his total delight in the imagination. For example, the consciousness of fear and isolation enunciated in the opening line are undercut by the conversational diction, loving tone, and gentle teasing humor of the remainder of the first two stanzas—allusions to Nadezhda's large mouth, and to her dauntless love, wit, courage and strength of character. Furthermore, the likely source of "nutpie" in line six reflects the concrete fact that the poem was inspired by Nadezhda's nameday celebration, which was made especially festive when her aunt arrived with a homemade nut torte.[3]

How much we have to fear, you and I,
Dearest big mouth, comrade mine!

Oh, how our tobacco crumbles,
Nutcracker, friend, idiot!

But would that, like a starling, I
Could whistle through life, eating nut pie. . . .

Clearly, there's no chance of that.
                                    (no. 202, 30 October 1930)

Stanza 3 ignores the stasis of the opening stanzas and soars in a flight of fancy, the vehicle for the speaker's humble vision of individual freedom and simple pleasures. That vision drifts off into three dots, however, and is severely undercut by the poem's extraordinarily powerful single-line conclusion, which jars reader and poem back to reality. Following his flight of fancy, this line emerges as an existential sigh. Thus, the motif of fear, presented in the first half, is countered in the second half by the introduction of the conditional mood, expressing the fantasy condition of the imagination as incantatory verbal magic: "But would that like a starling / I . . ." And even though the fantasy is broken off, it is the poetic imagination that provides the mythopoetic condition of this lyric, ensuring a moment of possibility, a disposition toward the future. In this way the poetic imagination again, as in "Fourth Prose" and *Journey to Armenia,* is associated with the conditional mood that elevates the poet, if but for a moment, above the fears and specters of this world. Mandelstam employed the conditional mood for purposes of incantation as one of a series of devices to defy fear and death, history and time.

Irony also functions to counterbalance fear for the future with the fantasy vision of an indulgent, carefree existence. Mandelstam's lyric voice had returned, emboldened by irony first mentioned as essential to poetic survival in his very early essay "François Villon" (1910)—"A pitiful vagabond, he attained for himself the unattainable aided only by his sharp irony." Years later, irony as a device of aesthetic intensity and as a moral weapon directed against his mortal enemies reached a climax in his Jeremiad, "Fourth Prose." Here, in the verse of the 1930s, irony sustains a new, self-conscious and self-mocking tonality associated with the speaker as witness of contemporary life. The poetic imagination—often represented by the conditional mood—in conjunction with irony appears to protect Mandelstam over the next eight years, helping him to defy reality, including bouts of physical illness, depression, and madness that almost overwhelmed him after his first arrest.

The sociopolitical impulses behind the attitudinal and stylistic changes in the later poetry may go back to the Eulenspiegel Affair of 1928–29, which provoked both Mandelstam's vitriolic exorcism of the literary establishment in "Fourth Prose" and his more contemplative *Journey to Armenia*. In the latter, the humble, hard-working common man, who has a "feeling for the fullness of life and . . . magnificent familiarity with the world of real things," is identified as prototypical of the human condition. The speaker of the *Moscow Notebooks* and *Voronezh Notebooks* identifies with the defiance of "Fourth Prose" and with the Armenian prototype alternately or simultaneously. Most important, the image of the autobiographically motivated lyric persona as vagabond, *raznochinets*, outcast, Jew, and prototype of the human condition helps to establish new poetic norms for the 1930s.[4]

The seemingly fragmented style and the use of dialogue in "How much we have to fear," as in many lyrics written in the 1930s, reflect Mandelstam's prose techniques. Moreover, like a number of his later poems, it contains an uneven number of lines (three- to seven-line poems are not uncommon), nonstandard lexicon, nontraditional rhyme patterns, and even unconventional combined meters. For example, the standard iambic tetrameter that opens "How much we have to fear" is unexpectedly interrupted in line 4 by a nonstandard meter—*dolniks*. This helps to form a complex metrical pattern in the poem as a whole.[5]

Lydia Ginzburg, in her essay on Mandelstam's poetics, provides arguments strikingly similar to Hartman's in *The Unmediated Vision* to justify the apparently unorthodox elements in the poet's later work. She notes that in viewing history as "the immediate present . . . [he could not use] conventional styles . . . [for they] were ill equipped to tackle contemporary life, to deal with the fluid, the incomplete, the as yet unnamed." Hence, she concludes, the themes and motifs of Mandelstam's new verse "emerge from unexpected impressions, thoughts, recollections, from any inner experience, bringing in tow everyday, prosaic words, signifying the diversity of contemporary reality. . . ."[6]

Most of Mandelstam's poems dating from October–November 1930 and written in Tbilisi at the end of his "two hundred days in the Sabbath land" express the poet's intense emotional response to Armenia which had come to represent his new poetic Covenant with "truth," his vow to reveal "the book of the earth."[7] Indeed, the antithesis he draws between Armenia and Soviet Russia in 1930–31 is fully integrated into his new mythopoesis. In one of the "Fragments of Destroyed Poems" (nos. 237–46), dated a year after his return from Armenia, the poet-speaker not only declares that he was "forcibly returned to Buddhist Moscow," but provides a clear opposition between Moscow, which exemplifies the new Soviet Age, and Armenia, which signifies his Covenant of "truth." In Mandelstam's lexicon, "Buddhist" stands for "apathy" and "inertia," recalling Alexander Herzen's depiction of Moscow as a city "in the sleep of lethargy":

> In the thirty-first year of this century
> I returned, no—read: I was forcibly
> Returned to Buddhist Moscow,
> But, I had just witnessed
> Rich Ararat spread out like a Biblical cloth,
> And spent *two hundred days in the Sabbath land*
> Known by the name of Armenia.
> If you're thirsty—what waters gush
> From the Kurdish source at Arzni—
> . . . *The waters of truth.* . . .
>> (no. 237, 1931; my italics)

Most significantly, however, the poet-persona reveals the fact that conscious self-renewal has given him the strength to challenge history— contemporary Soviet life and time itself. Having accepted his imperative, he is now determined to "speak for everyone":

> I am no longer a child. You, grave,
> You dare not teach a hunchback—be silent!
> I speak for everyone. My strength is such that
> My palate has become the heavens, my lips
> Have cracked open like the red clay earth.
>> (no. 240, 1931, Moscow)

The image of the poet's "lips" presented in "I have forgotten the word" has evolved into one of Mandelstam's most powerful emblems of poetic creation. It is still associated with the idea of pain and sacrifice as integral to the creative act. An analogy is drawn in the "Ar-

menian cycle" between the poet and the Armenian "earth": his lips
have "cracked open" like the "red clay earth." Mandelstam's "Fragments" echo his "Armenian cycle," where he first offered the image of
earth both as the book studied by its "original inhabitants" and as "the
ulcerous book" that torments the poet "like music and the word":

> And never again shall I discover
> In the library of clay authors
> The empty book of the magnificent earth,
> Studied by its original inhabitants.
> $\qquad$ (no. 214, October–November 1930)

> Azure and clay, clay and azure,
> What else . . . eyes . . . over . . .
> The book of sounding clay, the book of earth,
> Over the ulcerous book, the clay road,
> Which torments us like music and the word.
> $\qquad$ (no. 215, 16 September–5 November 1930, Tiflis)

The shock of Mandelstam's return to Soviet Russia turned out to be
far greater than he had anticipated. He encountered the most discon-
certing hostility not in "Buddhist Moscow," but in his beloved Leningrad, to which the Mandelstams, filled with naive hope, returned in
December 1930.

In her memoirs Nadezhda Mandelstam recalls that the Eulenspiegel
Affair still haunted Mandelstam; he was still regarded by the literary
establishment as persona non grata. When he approached Nikolay Tik-
honov at the Writers' Union requesting work and living space in the
Leningrad House of Writers, she remembers "the passionate conviction
in his voice as he said to us: 'Mandelstam shall not live in Leningrad.
We will not give him a room.'"[8]

Their misperception that they would be welcome in Leningrad cou-
pled with their need to reside temporarily with Mandelstam's brother
Evgeny, whom he later disowned because of his callousness, undoubtedly motivated the painful Leningrad poems of December 1930, no.
221, "I returned to my city . . ." ("Vernulsia v moi gorod . . .") and
January 1931, no. 223, "Help me, Lord . . ." ("Pomogi, Gospod'"),
and no. 225, "You and I will sit awhile in the kitchen" ("My s toboi
na kukhne posidim"), those unconstrained responses to an intolerable
experience.

The opening stanza of "I returned to my city, familiar to the point of tears, / . . . to the swollen glands of my childhood years," vividly contrasts the speaker's desperate search for reminders of his beloved city—nostalgia even for the illnesses and unpleasant aspects of his St. Petersburg childhood—with his gradual realization, in the latter half of the poem, that all connections between contemporary Leningrad and the St. Petersburg of his memory have vanished. The city is now a sinister Necropolis where people are either dead or anticipating death (stanzas 4–5):[9]

> Petersburg! I don't want to die yet.
> You have telephone numbers of mine.
>
> Petersburg! I still have addresses,
> At which I'll find the voices of the dead.

The brevity of "Help me, Lord"—a mere three lines—and its slow, heavy trochaic hexameter which, by omitting the unstressed syllables at the end of the third and sixth feet, emphasizes the speaker's fear and even his effort to pray, make this poem even more terrifying. He perceives "St. Petersburg / Leningrad" explicitly as a "grave," to which "v *grobu*" (in the grave), read as an anagrammatic or phonic transformation of the stressed syllable in "V Peter*burge*," provides subtle phonosemantic reinforcement:

> Help me, Lord, to live through this night:
> I fear for my life—the life of Your slave—
> To live in Petersburg is to sleep in the grave.
> (no. 223, January 1931)

> Pomogi, Gos*pod*', etu noch' pro*zhit*':
> Ia za zhizn' boi*us*'—za Tvoiu ra*bu*—
> V Peter*burge zhit*'—slovno spat' v gro*bu*.
> (my italics)

Finally, in the last poem Mandelstam would write in his beloved city, "We'll sit awhile in the kitchen," the speaker slowly reveals his sense of persecution. Contrary to the suggestion of simple domestic bliss implied in stanza 1, his ominous fate gradually unfolds. The image of the "sharp knife" in stanza 2, subtly initiates a sinister undertone that prefigures the anguish of the leave-taking: they must give up the warmth of the kitchen "before dawn," so as not to be tracked down:

We'll sit awhile in the kitchen.
The white kerosene smells sweet.

A sharp knife, and a large round loaf . . .
Pump up the primus stone, if you will,

Or else scrounge some string
To tie up our basket before dawn,

So we may leave for the station,
Where no one will seek us out.
                                                              (no. 225, January 1931)

The Moscow Experience

Housing in Moscow was not easy to obtain either, but by the summer of 1931 the Moscow Writers' Union had granted them a small squalid room in the Herzen House on Tverskoi Boulevard. Two years later, in the autumn of 1933, when Bukharin again intervened, they were assigned a small fourth-story apartment on Furmanov Lane, which became the subject of Mandelstam's strikingly derogatory attack on the Soviet system of mutual obligation, no. 272, "The apartment is silent, like paper" ("Kvartira tikha, kak bumaga"), one of a number of satirical poems written at this time.[10]

Despite its trials, this period proved extremely fruitful. The summer of 1931 produced not only *Journey to Armenia*, but the exceptionally witty and poignant Moscow cycle, including no. 260, "Midnight in Moscow" ("Polnoch' v Moskve"), no. 247, "Enough sulking! Stick the papers in the desk" ("Dovol'no kuksit'sia! Bumagi v stol zasunem"), nos. 237–40, "Fragments from destroyed poems," no. 265, "Today's the day for making decalcomanias" ("Segodnia mozhno sniat' dekal'-komani"), and no. 251, "I'm still far from being a patriarch" ("Eshche daleko mne do patriarkha"). This cycle concludes the first *Moscow Notebook* (October 1930–October 1931).

The basic subject of the Moscow cycle is the poet's effort to redefine his place in the Soviet era. Although highly critical of the new age, he expresses a genuine desire to reestablish himself within it personally and professionally. The themes of the age and time sounded in *1921–1925*, when he firmly denied being a "contemporary"—"No, never was I anyone's contemporary" (1924)— reappear, only now the poet's attitude, tone, language, rhythm, and worldview have radically shifted. An ironic tonality combined with a complex structure emphasizes his new mythopoesis.

"Midnight in Moscow" is a fine example of Mandelstam's attempt to disregard orthodox poetic conventions by treating the themes of the age and time in the context of contemporary life. Generically it is perhaps closer to the narrative poem, the *poema,* than the brief lyric. Its twelve stanzas of uneven length are organized through varied and alternating metrical, rhythmical, and rime patterns. Furthermore, Mandelstam attempts to interweave, juxtapose, and merge different forms of address and perspective, ranging from the impersonal third-person narration framing the poem to intimate first-person reminiscences on the one hand, and unconventional dialogue in the second-person singular on the other. Introducing dialogue and conversational idiom into a poetic structure that begins and ends more conventionally recalls his evaluation of oral communication defined in *Journey to Armenia* as "the warm light of oral instruction, the lucid didacticism of intimate conversation . . . far superior to the . . . homiletic function of books." Shifts in perspective are not always immediately apparent.

Although "Midnight in Moscow" is framed by the impersonal observations of a speaker particularly desirous of depicting the sounds and movements of contemporary urban life, the poem's dominant perspective is that of an autobiographically oriented eyewitness. While the third-person frame unifies the seemingly haphazard structure of the poem's twelve stanzas, which at first seem to vary radically in poetic format and point of view, the eyewitness perspective unifies the poem thematically, for in stanza 8 the speaker confesses he *is* a "contemporary," for he is not only an inhabitant of the new capital city, but his jacket bears "the *Moskvoshveiia* label."[11] He thus confirms that his presence in Moscow is analogous to his status as a "contemporary" and that his role is defined by his moral allegiance to the "fourth estate." Even though this confession is not elicited until the poem's final third, its striking emotional power anchors the work's entire perspective. The confession is evoked through both gentle self-mockery and serious mockery of the state or the establishment, the latter being expressed in the speaker's challenge "just try to wrench me out of the age."

    (1) Midnight in Moscow. A luxurious Buddhist summer.
        The streets diverge, finely tapping their narrow steel-
        tipped boots.

(2) Boulevard rings grow blissful in their black smallpox;
    Moscow's never quiet even at night.
    When peace darts out from under hooves,
    You'll say: somewhere over there on the firing range
    Two clowns have made their lodgings, Bim and Bom,
    They've set little hammers and combs going.
    Now a mouth organ sounds,
    Now a child's toy piano—
    Do-re-mi-fa,
    Sol-fa-mi-re-do. . . .

(3) Time was, when I was younger,
    I'd go out in a patched up raincoat,
    Into the open arms of the boulevards
    Where a little gypsy girl's matchstick legs
    Struck her long skirts, where the trained bear—
    Nature's own eternal Menshevik—strolled.
    And how fragrant the cherry-laurels. . . .
    Where are you off to? The laurels are gone, the cherries. . . .

(4) I'll tighten up the mechanism
    On the runaway kitchen clock.
    Ah, how rugged time is,
    Just the same, I love chasing its tail:
    After all, it can't be blamed for running as it does,
    And anyway its just a bit of a prankster.

(5) Get away from me! Stop your begging, stop complaining!
    Shut up! Stop whimpering!
               Is that what the *raznochintsy* stamped
    Their cracked boots for, that I should betray them now?
    We shall die, like foot-soldiers,
    But we shall glorify neither theft, nor daylabor, nor lies!

(6) A spiderweb's left of our old Scottish laprobe—
    You'll drape it over me like a military flag, when I die.
    Let's drink, old friend, to our barley malt grief,—
    Bottoms up! . . .

(7) From darkened movie theaters
    Crowds deadened, as if overdosed on chloroform,
    Exit. How venous they are,
    And how desperate for oxygen!

(8) It's time you know, I'm also a contemporary,
    I'm a man bearing the *Moskvosheviia* label,
    Look how my jacket puffs up on me,
    How I've learned to strut and speak!
    Just try to wrench me out of the age!—
    I guarantee you'll wring your own neck!

(9) I speak with the age, but does it really
    Have a hempen soul,
    Have we really begotten a bastard,
    Like some wrinkled little beast in a Tibetan temple—
    Scratching itself before jumping into a zinc tub—
    Show us some more, Marya Ivanna!

(10) This may be insulting, but get this:
     There's labor lechery, and we've got it in our blood.

(11) It's already growing light. Gardens hum like a green telegraph.
     Raphael is coming to visit Rembrandt.
     He and Mozart adore Moscow—
     For its hazel eyes and the intoxication of a summer night.

(12) And like pneumatic mail
     Or Black Sea jellyfish aspic
     Draughts of air circulate from apartment
     To apartment by air conveyor,
     Like free-loading students in May. . . .

The pseudolyricism that opens stanzas 1 and 2—and in particular the potentially lyrical atmosphere implied by "luxurious summer" (1.1–2) and the metonymic "boulevard rings" that "grow blissful" (2.1–2)—is clearly undermined by the negative epithets "Buddhist" and "in black smallpox," which impose the speaker's discomfort on the unquiet capital (2.3).

Moreover, this pseudolyricism is soon countered by the imagined dialogue and nostalgic reminiscences inserted into the third-person narration. Introduced by "You'll say," the dialogue suggests the reasons for Moscow's "never being quiet" (2.4–11) in emotionally charged, phonically reflective childhood recollections combining infantile language, musical instruments, and scales. These reminiscences provide the impetus for stanza 3, in which the speaker fully realizes the first-person autobiographical mode, and concludes on a note of elegiac yearning (3.1–7). Nevertheless, another shift to the intimate form of address ("Where are you going?") might imply the continuation of the dialogue initiated in stanza 2, as might the first-person singular statement that opens stanza 4, suggesting a response to a domestic request.

Stanza 4 treats the theme of "time" more overtly, indicating an attempt to control it within the frame of intimate dialogue (4.3–6). Time is even personified as an elusive practical joker with whom the speaker enjoys playing chase games. The intimate, humorous, and ironic tone of the dialogue is sustained.

The conversational idiom dominating the intimate "I"–"You" relationship differs markedly from the pseudolyrical idiom of the distant third-person narration. But the conversational idiom itself also varies. The highly colloquial language introducing stanza 3 is replaced by crude and vulgar language in stanza 5, a speech shift that reflects the shift in addressee. The intimate companion of the earlier dialogue is replaced by the self, as the speaker attempts to define his stance toward the contemporary Soviet state (5.1–4). Defiance of the state is juxtaposed to his allegiance to the *raznochintsy,* that group of critical intellectuals and social misfits with whom Mandelstam continually declared his spiritual affinity from *Noise of Time* to *Conversation about Dante.* In his lexicon, the *raznochintsy* as standard bearers of moral truth and spiritual power, represented a creative challenge to the status quo, a source of ethical and aesthetic renewal.

Indeed, when the first-person singular yields to the plural in the concluding lines of stanza 5 (5.5–6), the subject matter, intonation, and language are elevated. Anger and defiance give way to acceptance of a new role. The individual witness ("I"), having acknowledged his position, becomes the spokesman for his generation ("We"), a role Mandelstam would maintain in the *Voronezh Notebooks*: thus, it is uncanny how the line "We will die like foot-soldiers" prefigures his major poetic cycle of 1937, "Verses on the Unknown Soldier."

Although it is not until the ninth stanza that the poet-persona confirms through the autobiographical mode his intention to "speak with the age," he implies a moral right to speak for his generation in rejecting lines from his own earlier poem: "The Dawn / Dusk of Freedom." The last lines of stanza 5, "We shall die like foot-soldiers / But we shall glorify neither theft, nor daylabor, nor lies!," counters the first-person plural imperative voice of 1917 which urged his "Brothers" to "glorify the fateful" age:[12]

Let us glorify, brothers, the dawn/dusk of freedom. . . .

Let us glorify the fateful burden
Which the people's leader assumes in tears
Let us glorify the somber burden of power,
Its intolerable weight.

Stanza 6, continuing in the first-person plural, suggests the speaker's preparations for death as a soldier sharing the common destiny of his age. Here, however, the plural subtly shifts into intimate dialogue as he requests his companion to "drape" his coffin, using their old laprug "like a military flag." Having acknowledged his fate, he enjoins his companion to drink with him (6.3–4), thus reverting to the domestic intimacy and fear for the future shared with his companion in such lyrics as "How much we have to fear" and "We'll sit awhile in the kitchen."

After the poet toasts his destiny, the dialogue ends in three dots, replaced once more by third-person eyewitness reportage in stanza 7. However, the impersonal description of Moscow's "dead" or "deadened" inhabitants is personalized by emotional exclamations noting "how desperate they are for oxygen," that is, for freedom and change. The twice repeated colloquialism "how [much]" (*do chego*) reveals the speaker's empathy with that public desperation.

This is followed by the deeply personal confession of stanza 8. In both 8 and 9, the speaker turns again to the first-person singular, but no longer in the form of nostalgic reminiscences or self-inquiry. Rather, self-mocking confession elicits his most affirmative statements about his relationship to contemporaneity: "I'm a contemporary too," "I speak with the age." In stanza 9, in highly colloquial language and a mocking tone, the speaker questions his own understanding of the "soul" of the age, personified as "bastard" and "beast" (*zverek*). And the two-line stanza that follows continues the tone of the confession, stressing his right to bear witness even though his views "may be insulting" (10.1–2).

The concluding stanzas return to the third-person perspective. The poet reaffirms his faith in organic and cultural continuity even in the *Moskvoshveiia* era (10), and, in the future, in the reemergence of "light" (11.1) and "air" (12), enlightenment and freedom. The voice of "the new intermediary" thus speaks simultaneously from within—first-person perspective—and from without—third-person narration. His conclusion suggests that organic growth, cultural memory, faith in life and in the future, may, after all, conquer time.

In "I'm still far from being a patriarch," the speaker—mouthing colloquial, self-reflexive dialogue—asserts his intransigence (1), contemplates "what binds [him] to the world" (2), and details the possibilities for human satisfaction in Moscow (3, 8).

> "You so-and-so!" Well, what of it, I beg your pardon,
> But down deep nothing in me is changed. . . . (1)
>
> When you think what binds you to the world,
> You don't believe it yourself: it's nonsense. . . . (2)
>
> I laugh sometimes, or shily assume a dignified air,
> And picking up my walking stick, go out—
> I listen to sonatas in alleyways,
> And lick my lips at vendors' wares,
> I leaf through books in stonefaced entryways,
> And although I'm not alive, yet I am alive. (3)
>
> I love the starling-streetcar departures,
> And the asphalt's Astrakhan caviar. . . . (8)

Nevertheless, in the final stanza we learn that neither the new nor the exotic satisfies fundamental human needs:

> How much I'd like to express my feelings,
> Speak my mind, spurt out the truth,
> Send spleen to the devil, to hell;
> I'd like to take someone's hand: "Be so kind,"
> I'd say, "I think we're going the same way. . . ." (10)

Conversation about Dante

Approximately eight months elapsed between the first and second *Moscow Notebooks*. Though in 1930–1931 the poet voiced his desire to reestablish his allegiance to the "fourth estate,"[13] the second *Moscow Notebook* (May 1932–February 1934) contains some of his most negative satirical verse. Nevertheless, like *Conversation about Dante* it focuses primarily on themes of the poet and poetic creation.[14]

Conversation about Dante, an exposition of Mandelstam's poetic credo, was written during the summer of 1933 at the Koktebel' writer's rest home in the Crimea, where by happy coincidence Andrey Bely was working on a treatise on Gogol. A stimulating friendship ensued, for each poet was deeply involved in an effort to convey to his readers the essence of poetic creation as expressed by a master of world literature, while simultaneously discoursing on his own experience as poet and reader. A few months later, Mandelstam initiated a lyric statement of his poetic credo in "The Octets."

While *Conversation about Dante* is a counterpart to *Journey to Armenia* thematically and structurally, it emphasizes what Mandelstam termed "the instinct for form creation" or "the impulse" behind the text as the source of immortality in art. It focuses on the relationship between the impulse to preserve the eternal verities through human creativity and the phenomenon of the perpetuation of art through generations of readers.

Although Mandelstam first mentioned "oral instruction" and the "physiology of reading" in *Journey to Armenia,* only in *Conversation about Dante* does he offer his own experience reading an immortal text. The originality of this essay derives from his focus on the ideal reader. Oriented toward active intuition of the impulses behind poetic genius, Mandelstam's external model is Dante, his internal experience—his own "creative cognition": "I am engaged in a struggle to make the work comprehensible as an entity, to graphically demonstrate that which is conceivable. Only through metaphor is it possible to find a concrete sign to represent the instinct for form creation by which Dante accumulated and poured forth his *terza rima"* (*SS,* 376; *CPL,* 409).

In *Conversation about Dante,* then, Mandelstam endeavors both to demonstrate what makes Dante a "master of the instruments of poetry" and to convey how the mind of the creative artist transforms original creative impulses into living poetry. He employs "oral instruction" to pursuade the reader to allow his own imagination to respond intuitively to the dynamics of the creative process which, for Mandelstam, *is* the poetic text.

As *Conversation about Dante* develops, we move from metaphorical definitions into Dante's text itself, focusing on poetic consciousness as we enter the arena of the "performance."

Mandelstam first attempts to establish a new definition of poetry or "poetic discourse" to supersede the current clichès of literary criticism. He asserts that poetry is unique because it is always in process, indeed always part of a "hybrid process." For Mandelstam, "hybridization" was an organic phenomenon essential to the creative process, an integral element of literary form that assured the proper union of memory and the imagination.

Furthermore, just as *Journey to Armenia* shows how Mandelstam's imperative is enacted by the poet—how he *becomes* his own imperative, the "verb on horseback"—so *Conversation about Dante* demonstrates how the essence of poetry subsists in "performance," for poetry does not reflect, or tell about, life, but "enacts life" (*razygrivaet zhizn'*). Since poetry is autonomous, it "establishes itself with astonishing independence in a new extraspatial field of action, not so much narrating as acting out nature by means of its arsenal of devices. . . ." Indeed, Mandelstam attempts to create the impression that a poem is actually a piece of human fate, not merely a reflection of it or even a narrative about it. His later poems are thus "enactments" of states of mind, events, or intuitions, and the fragmented nature of some of them may be due to the fact that they are intended as "unedited" enactments—spontaneous impulses embodied in words.

Thus Mandelstam maintains that "What is important in poetry is *only* the understanding which brings it about, or the impulse—certainly not the passive, reproducing, or paraphrasing understanding," for "meaning" can be grasped only through metaphor. Otherwise it is inexplicable, unparaphrasable:

The quality of poetry is determined by the speed and decisiveness with which it embodies its schemes and commands in diction, the instrumentless, lexical, purely quantitative verbal matter. One must traverse the full width of a river crammed with Chinese junks moving simultaneously in various directions—thus the meaning of poetic speech is created. This meaning, the itinerary, cannot be reconstructed by interrogating the boatmen: they will not be able to tell how and why we were jumping from junk to junk. (*SS*, 2:364–65; *CPL*, 398)

A great poet, then, must be judged by his mastery of "the instruments of poetic discourse." Examples include Blok, who "sensed the life of language and literary forms . . . as hybridization," and Dante, the "strategist of transmutation and hybridization."

Conversation about Dante differs from Mandelstam's early essays in that it contains numerous autobiographical digressions. He contemplates his personal, emotional, and often physiological "love of the word," his fascination with verbal texture, phonosemantics, and the relationship between the impulse and the text. His personal recollections even reflect his awareness of the physiological nexus between poet and poem: "The mouth works, the smile nudges the line of verse, cleverly and gaily the lips redden, the tongue trustingly presses itself against the palate."

Physiological consciousness is also an integral part of Mandelstam's unique philological approach to reading poetry and to reeducating the reader: "We must give examples of Dante's rhythms. People are ignorant of this. . . . [He glorifies] the human gait, the measure and rhythm of walking, footstep and form. The step, linked to breathing and saturated with thought, Dante understood as the beginning of prosody . . . the metrical foot is its inhalation and exhalation. Each step concludes, invigorates, syllogizes" (SS, 2:366–67; *CPL,* 400).

In addition to his incisive remarks on rhythm and movement, Mandelstam discusses Dante's use of tense in an astonishingly original manner, one that recalls his own careful juxtaposition of grammatical forms. He indicates how particular elements of poetic discourse acquire semantic significance and thereby distinguish poetic discourse from automatic everyday speech formations. He attempts to demonstrate how "any process involving the creation of form in poetry presupposes lines, periods or cycles of sound forms, as is the case with individually enunciated semantic units."

Other motifs persisting in the work of both poets include the quest for precision of perception and clarity of understanding, the concept of space or spatial form, and of course, the idea of metamorphosis and recurrence. He selected Dante as the subject of this conversation, Mandelstam claims, "because he is the greatest, the unrivaled master of transformable and convertible poetic matter."

Mandelstam, then, is hardly speaking only about Dante. His autobiographical mediation strongly influences his interpretation. He links Dante to his own self-image as the idealized *raznochinets*-philologist in *Noise of Time* and his pledge to the *raznochintsy* in "Midnight in Moscow":

Dante is a poor man . . . an internal *raznochinets* . . . [who] does not know how to behave . . . I am not imagining this; I infer it from the numerous admissions of Alighieri himself.

The inner anxiety and . . . gaucheries which accompany each step of the diffident man . . . untutored in ways of applying his inner experience or of objectifying it in etiquette, tormented and outcast, such qualities . . . provide the poem with all its charm, its drama . . . its psychological foundation. (*SS,* 2:372; *CPL,* 405)

Thus, in contrast to the immature and egocentric author of "Morning of Acmeism" (1913), who focused on the "rules" for poetry making, on craft rather than "performance," the mature poet of the 1930s contemplates the impulse to creation and the dynamics of the poetic process in a text which has withstood the test of time.

"The Octets"

A few months later Mandelstam began "The Octets" (nos. 275–85, "Vos'mistishiia"), a poetic cycle illuminating both as a lyrical restatement of his poetic credo and as a window into his method of poetic creation. Although most of the cycle was composed in November 1933 (nos. 276–77, 280–83), he refused to record them on paper until January 1934, when he was moved by the death of Andrey Bely to pay him tribute. In February he recorded one of his poems to Bely (no. 279) and another eight-line poem from 1932 (no. 278), incorporating them into "The Octets." However, it was not until July 1935, after he had already spent a year in exile in Voronezh, that he composed the poem that now opens the cycle (no. 275, a "twin" of no. 276) and recorded his last two octets (nos. 284–85). According to Nadezhda Mandelstam, except for the first three poems, the final order of the cycle was never authorized.[15]

While "The Octets" contain numerous phonic and semantic bonds, they are unified above all by Mandelstam's complex imagery transformed through phonosemantic, syntactic, and rhythmical connections. Rational or temporal sequence is less significant than intuitively grasped and internally bonded images. The fluid order of the cycle reflects an important precept of his later poetics, the idea that poetry is not merely what is recorded on paper, but a fluid process of continuous "performance."[16]

Mandelstam's imperative, simultaneously aesthetic-metaphysical and moral-autobiographical, has its source in his mythopoetic vision of cultural and historical synchrony which, in his role as "the new intermediary," he is enjoined to preserve and transmit to the "reader in posterity." As is shown in "The Octets," the poet-speaker is endowed with extraordinary powers to communicate with future generations—a "sixth sense," supersensory perception, a capacity to penetrate Nature's laws. And, as master of transformation and transmission, the poet-speaker can cross with impunity the boundaries between history and infinity.

The opening "twin" octets (nos. 275–76), introduce us first to the speaker's enjoyment of the creative process itself—"I love to watch the fabric [of poetry] form"—despite the physical difficulties and pain accompanying poetic creation.

Second, we find that the poet's highly complex relationship with the metaphysical realm is expressed in imagery that unites his two major fields of images: the "child" (innocence, intuition, spontaneity, biological and creative potential, futurity, and indeed, teleology) and "space" (the void, emptiness, open expanses, the heavens, and infinity). It is significant that Mandelstam revised his opening octet to link these two images, and that their bond is generated through the motif of poetic creation. In the later octets the linkage is less stable and more complex (nos. 279, 284), though the fundamental motifs are reiterated. Innocence, intuition, spontaneity, and teleology remain essential to "creative cognition":

> I love to watch the fabric form
> When after two or three
> Or even four gasps
> There comes the rectifying sigh—
> And sketching open forms
> With the arcs regattas make,
> Space plays half-awake—
> A child who's never known the cradle.
> (no. 275, November 1933, Moscow—July 1935, Voronezh)

In subsequent octets the image of the child is associated with teleological design, with striving to grow and to "comprehend the inner excess of space" (no. 279), with continuity of the universe and future potential (no. 284). Mandelstam's concept of organic growth and autonomous development, in his work a teleological premise, also links "the child" with the "colossal roots" of the last octet (no. 285), which signify not only mathematical and metaphysical roots (connected through "magnitudes"), but biological roots (connected with gardens, plants, natural phenomena), word-roots (connected with the phonosemantic relationships involving assonance, rhyme, grammatical categories, syntactical parallelisms), and in general, all sources of "the Word" or Logos. Thus, the child as "the premature fetus" and, metaphorically, the as yet unborn poem striving "to become" (no. 279), is again associated with the origins of poetic creation, with organic, sci-

entific, poetic, and teleological unfolding, not with "contemporary
theories of development":

> Having conquered Nature's rote learning,
> The hard blue eye penetrated its laws,
> Inside the earth's crust rocks act like holy fools,
> And a moan is torn from its breast like ore.
> The premature fetus is propelled
> As if along a spiral-shaped pathway—
> To comprehend the inner excess of space,
> And the pledge of petal and cupola.
>   (no. 279, January 1934, Moscow)

A highly significant element in this octet, originally part of the
cycle on Bely's death, is the use of the propulsion metaphor which, in
Journey to Armenia, signifies the poet's imperative. Here the premature
fetus-poem is "propelled" (*tianetsia*) along the "horn-" or spiral-shaped
road of life. And the analogy here between the poetic process and the
growth process again recalls *Journey to Armenia*: "the very process of
remembering, crowned with the victory of memory's effort, is astonishingly similar to the phenomenon of growth."

Both poetic creation and poem, presented as process and promise,
pledge to fill empty space with human consciousness—values, ideals,
memories and prophecies. The poetic process moves beyond mere imitation ("the rote learning" ascribed to nature) and penetrates the earth
to discover nature's "laws." The emergent poem gradually follows its
autonomous path, fulfilling its promise. The poetic process thus demonstrates teleological order, which the poet-speaker communicates to
the "reader in posterity" through the "pledge of petal and cupola."

Indeed, the fifth octet (no. 279) also provides a fine example of the
poet's phonosemantic strategies, indicating how Mandelstam's intuition of the interconnectedness of word-roots has come to dominate his
poetry since *Tristia* ("I have forgotten the word"), and how the resultant patterns emphasize his mythopoetic vision of teleological design.
We find not only phonic inversions of word-roots, as in -*rod*- from
pri*rod*a (Nature), iu*rod*stvuet (act/live the life of the holy fool), and
po*rod*y (species, rocks), inverted to read -*do*[*r*]- in ne*dor*azvitok (premature fetus) and *dor*ogoi (road, path), but a host of "transmutations
and hybridizations" derived from a given root and its phonic relations.
For example, -*rod*- and *ruda*/*grudy* (ore/beast), or -*rod*- and *rog* (horn)
and *dor*ogoi (by the road), which includes both *dor*- and *rog*-. In addi-

tion, bonds are developed through rhymes—internal rhymes, full and truncated rhymes, rhymes with displaced consonants, assonance and anaphora. Furthermore, numerous semantic associations emerge through prefixes, such as *za-* in *za*kon (law) and *za*log (pledge), or *pre-*, *pri-*, *pro-*, and *po-*: *Pre*odolev (overcome, surmount), *pro*nik (penetrated), *pro*stranstvo (space, void, emptiness), *pri*roda (nature), *po*rody (species, rocks), and *po*niat' (to understand, comprehend):

*Pre*odolev za*tverzh*ennost' pri*rod*y,	pre-, -rod-, tverzh
Golubo*tverd*yi glaz *pro*nik ee *za*kon,	za-, tverd-, pro-
V zemnoi kore iu*rod*stvuiut po*rod*y,	-rod-
I kak *rud*a iz *grud*i rvetsia ston.	rud-
I tianetsia glukhoi ne*dor*azvitok,	-dor-
Kak by, *dor*ogoi, so*g*nutoiu v *rod*,--	dor-, rog-, og, rod
*Po*niat' *pro*stranstva vnutrennii izbytok	po-, pro,
I lepestka i kupola *za*log.	za-

These relationships "enact" the fluid process of continuous creation or "performance" discussed in *Conversation about Dante,* for the reader experiences the continuous and intricate interchange of meanings as his eye moves from word to word, line to line, and his ear recognizes patterns from sound to sound.

Finally, in the last two octets (284–85), we find not only a sharp attack on theories of causality as illusory—which recalls the condemnation in "On the Nature of the Word" and *Journey to Armenia* of contemporary theories of evolution and determinism—but also the counterposition of the image of organic and creative potential—the teleological image of the child—to the negative images of causality and constancy. Thus, even though the speaker asserts that "we" adults are intoxicated by the illusions of causality (no. 284), "the child" preserves in his very being "the great universe"; his "small eternity" contains mankind's future. What is more, since the future is potential, it is yet free of the deceptions plaguing the contemporary adult world with its ceaseless efforts to establish "causes;" "the child preserves his silence."

"Space," a far more complex image in Mandelstam's work, contains both negative and positive connotations. Its negative aspect is associated with emptiness, the void, lack of consciousness and control. Nevertheless, since the verse of *Stone* its openness has served the poet as an impulse to creation, for "space" demands to be filled: it challenges, summons, and invites. Human consciousness—in the forms created by the poet—responds.

The last octet (no. 285) depicts the poet's exit from "space" and his entrance into the "overgrown garden of magnitudes," where he comes into direct contact with illusions of constancy and causality:

> And I take leave of space and enter
> The overgrown garden of magnitudes,
> Where I tear to shreds sham constancy
> And the consciousness of causes.
> And your text, infinity,
> I read alone, without other people—
> Your leafless, wild book of nostrums,—
> A workbook of colossal roots.

Mandelstam's metaphysics, like Bergson's earlier, emphasizes intuition and instinct ("creative cognition" in *Journey to Armenia,* "instinct for form creation" in *Conversation about Dante*) as the source of truth and, consequently, of aesthetic cognition. The contemporary world, the "overgrown garden of magnitudes," with its abstract concepts and delusions, is now recognized as just as much of a challenge by the poet-speaker as empty space. The implication here seems to be that having challenged space and conquered its emptiness with "the pledge of petal and cupola," the poet-persona must now be prepared to face the contemporary world, to destroy its illusions of constancy and reject its abstract theories of causality, thereby upholding the eternal values, the "colossal roots" of "infinity's text."

Mandelstam's challenge to the contemporary world, however, almost silenced him, for on 13 May 1934 he was abruptly arrested. The poetic voice of the prolific Moscow years would, however, be reclaimed a year later in exile in Voronezh.

Chapter Eight
Voronezh Notebooks

I am in the heart of the age—the way is unclear
And time distances the goal. . .
(no. 332, 14 December 1936)

People need light and blue air,
They need bread and the snows of Elbrus. . . .
People need poetry secretly their own
To keep them awake forever. . .
To bathe them in its breath.
(no. 355, 19 January 1937)

Mandelstam's arrest and interrogation, his mental anguish and suicide attempt, his exile and the intervention on his behalf of such major figures as Bukharin and Pasternak,[1] followed by the subsequent "miracle"—Stalin's commutation of his sentence to "isolate but preserve," three years of exile in the southern Russian city of Voronezh rather than execution—left their mark on the poet's consciousness and profoundly affected his poetic voice. The shocking events of his private life, however, seem to have strengthened rather than diminished his self-image by reaffirming his faith in the vital role of the poet and poetry. New themes emerge, including, above all, faith in the power and joy of poetry as well as a somewhat mystical adherence to the idea of sharing in the destiny of the common man. Older themes continue in new forms—for example, the imminence of death. Mandelstam's last year in exile testifies to his renewed understanding of poetry as meeting a basic human need—"People need poetry . . . to keep them awake forever"—and discloses his profound sense of his own role as witness on the battlefield of human destiny ("Verses on the Unknown Soldier").

Lydia Ginzburg's remark that "Mandelstam's poetry always has its source at the point where fear of life and love of life meet"[2] is an extraordinarily apt summation of the "impulses" behind the complex texts we know as the *Voronezh Notebooks*.[3] Such "impulses," to use Mandelstam's own terminology from *Conversation about Dante,* not only in-

121

spired his most powerful verse, but generated the dense and seemingly obtuse quality of the later poetry.[4] Intimate personal reflections ("I am in the heart of the age—the way is unclear") refer directly to that crossroads "where fear of life and love of life meet," for it is there that the poet-speaker's personal-psychological self confronts the experience of his sociopolitical and metaphysical being. Indeed, in the *Voronezh Notebooks* Mandelstam's role as "intermediary" intensified tenfold as "personal experience" literally became his "sole authority and source of conviction."[5]

Oddly enough, the years of Voronezh exile proved even more prolific than the Moscow years. The collections of this period include the *First Voronezh Notebook* (April–July, 1935); the *Second Voronezh Notebook* (December 1936–February 1937), followed almost immediately by the *Third Voronezh Notebook* (March–May 1937).[6]

While the poetry of the *First Notebook* often expresses the poet-speaker's passion for the simple joys of human existence, consciousness of his reprieve as an unexpected gift of life may have simultaneously stimulated ambivalent feelings of guilt as well as some subconscious drive to pay for that gift. Such feelings may have led to the year and a half of silence preceding the *Second Notebook* and to the self-conscious decision to write an "Ode to Stalin" in which his own destiny is mystically linked to that of his tormentor through the phonosemantic "axis" (*os'*) of their given names—"*Os*ip" is a form of Stalin's name, "*Jos*eph."[7] The *Third Voronezh Notebook,* which contains extremes of Mandelstam's ecstatic and tragic vision, culminates in his ultimate farewell to mankind: "Verses on the Unknown Soldier."

The poem most frequently cited as having caused Mandelstam's arrest—the "Stalin Epigram"—was one of several satirical poems written toward the end of 1933. It was read, according to Nadezhda Yakovlevna, "to a number of people—eleven all told, including me, our brothers and Akhmatova. . . . Apart from the eleven named at the interrogation, seven or eight other people, including Shklovsky and Pasternak, had heard the poem. . . ."[8] One of them was obviously an informer:

> Our lives no longer feel ground under them.
> At ten paces you can't hear our words.
>
> But whenever there's a snatch of talk
> it turns to the Kremlin mountaineer,

the ten thick worms his fingers,
his words like measures of weight,

the huge laughing cockroaches on his top lip,
the glitter of his boot-rims.

Ringed with a scum of chicken-necked bosses
he toys with the tributes of half-men.

One whistles, another meows, a third snivels.
He pokes out his finger and he alone goes boom.

He forges decrees in a line like horseshoes,
One for the groin, one the forehead, temple, eye.

He rolls the executions on his tongue like berries.
He wishes he could hug them like big friends from home.
    (no. 286, November 1933; trans. Brown and Merwin)[9]

The "Epigram" contains the most explicit expression of Mandelstam's moral hostility toward the political cynicism of the age implied in his Moscow cycle, and in particular in the "Wolf" poem of 1931,[10] which included the lines:

The wolfhound age springs at my shoulders
though I'm no wolf by blood.
Better to be stuffed up a sleeve like a fleece cap
in a fur coat from the steppes of Siberia,

and so not see the snivelling, nor the sickly smears,
nor the bloody bones on the wheel,
so all night the blue foxes would still gleam
for me as they did in the first times.

Lead me into the night by the Yenesei
where the pine touches the star.
I'm no wolf by blood,
and only my own kind will kill me.
    (no. 227, 17–28 March 1931; trans. Brown and Merwin)

Although the "Wolf" poem clearly charges that men have abandoned moral values, it falls short of being a full-blown attack on the system or on Stalin. By 1933, however, Mandelstam's explicit anti-Soviet statements in "The Apartment is Silent as Paper" and the anti-Stalin "Epigram" were apparently enough to cause his arrest. Moreover, the political climate changed radically. Dissent was no longer merely challenged in the media. In 1929 Bukharin could intervene with the literary establishment over the trumped up "plagiarism" charges against Mandelstam and extricate him from the "Eulenspiegel Affair," but in 1934 he had to appeal to Stalin himself. By 1938, no one remained to help.

During the 1930s, the poet's life became his primary lyric material, as distinct from the monuments of human culture he apostrophized so magnificently in the early volumes, or the more abstruse, man-centered meditations on time, conscience, the poet and the age dominating *1921–1925*. However, the intense irony, even self-mockery of the *Moscow Notebooks* was somewhat toned down in the *Voronezh Notebooks,* although the general tonality established in the Moscow years remained.

Both the *Moscow Notebooks* and *Voronezh Notebooks* contain direct, impetuous, and poignant utterances. Exuberant exclamations of delight in the unexpected, in the joys of being alive coexist with frightening visions of the present and future; intimate revelations of the poet's need for warmth and beauty in this world are accompanied by firm declarations of fortitude and courage; oracular, prophetic, and mystical intimations of the future challenge Soviet reality and time itself. The seeming immediacy of shared involvement and the illusion of direct, intimate, and colloquial conversation temper the distance of unambiguous self-confidence, the aesthetic ambiguity of the meditative thinker, and the outrage of the polemicist. The voice of the persona as friend, companion, lover, and, above all, eyewitness, rejoices, rages, fears, despairs, reflects, testifies, judges, and prophesies. The poetry of the 1930s, then, alternates Mandelstam's inimitable spirit of love and defiance with his tragic vision—prescience of his own death, the death of world culture, and the death of humankind. While thematically and metaphorically the *Moscow Notebooks* and *Voronezh Notebooks* continue to record the signs in the universe signaling that all is not lost and the imperatives of the human soul that cannot be denied, structurally they are defined by a verbal texture richer and denser than that of any previous Russian poet. A limpid precision, sharpness of focus, and a vivid, dynamic inner mobility grace the lyrics of maturity with an elegant grandeur rarely encountered in twentieth-century verse.

"Black Earth"

"Black Earth" ("Chernozem," no. 299), the poem which opens the *Voronezh Notebooks,* was written in April 1935. It is a hymn in praise of the rich black earth of the Voronezh region. It is significant that this poem develops two major themes and fields of imagery from the 1920s and 1930s. On the one hand, the theme of the earth as the raw material and renewable source of poetic creation (the motif of "ploughed earth" from *Tristia* and the essay "Word and Culture") is blended with the motifs and imagery of the inexorable "book-like earth" of the Armenian cycle.[11] While these self-reminiscences emphasize the earth as the ultimate source of the creative process, Mandelstam goes one step further in "Black Earth" and the "Black Earth" cycle by inscribing the poet himself into his image of the earth.

Nevertheless, it is the subtle introduction of the second major theme—through the seemingly superficial analogy between the Voronezh hills and horses' withers in stanza 1—that actually makes possible the inscription of the poet, or rather his poetic imperative, into the image of the earth. In "Black Earth," the association of the earth—the rolling steppes—with horses' withers suggests self-reminiscence to the poet's imperative—the "verb on horseback"—depicted in *Journey to Armenia.*[12] This theme, although merely suggested here, is more fully developed two years later in no. 365, "I sing when my throat is moist . . ." ("Poiu kogda gortan' syra . . .," 8 February 1937).

So esteemed, so richly black, all in peak condition,
All in the little withers, all clean air and grooming,
All crumbly, all forming a chorus—
Moist clods of my earth and freedom!

In the days of early ploughing—black verging on blue,
Its inner work establishes itself unarmed—
A thousand hills of ploughed-up words—
It seems something's not surrounding our environs!

All the same the earth's a blunder and a butt—
You can't plead with it, or fall at its feet:
Like a decaying flute it alerts your hearing,
Like a matutinal clarinet it nips your ear like frost.

> How pleasing the thick rich layers on the ploughshare,
> How the steppe is silent in April's turning of the soil . . .
> Well, hello there, black-earth, be brave, open your eyes—
> There's black-eloquent silence in your work.
>
> (no. 299, April 1935)

Stylistically, both the imagery and unusual diction of "Black Earth" develop tendencies initiated in the Armenian and Moscow cycles. Although untypical of early Mandelstam, the conjunction of numerous neologisms with obsolete and colloquial expressions adds an original philological texture to the physical imagery of the later poetry, making translation extremely difficult. For instance, by reiterating the word *vsia* (*all,* whole, fully, totally) five times, the first stanza emphasizes the unity of the poet-speaker's view over the rolling hills of rich black earth spread out before him like well-groomed horses' withers; indeed, he seems to contemplate the way the earth's contours resemble the bare back of the horse he might ride. Simultaneously, this vision of unity and fullness is contrasted to its "crumbling" units, its "moist clods," praised equally for "crumbling" and for "forming a chorus." What is more, the apostrophized "moist clods" are highly personalized through the personal pronominal adjective, "*my,*" applied to "earth and freedom." Thus, something more than a hymn to the landscape is suggested.

Indeed, the elevated tone of the introductory adjectives—neologisms signifying rhetoric of extreme praise—"most thoroughly esteemed" (*pereuvazhena*) and "most thoroughly or richly black" (*perecherna*), but also possibly suggesting "overly esteemed" and "overly black" in a context of excessive repetition—implies that Mandelstam's hymn may be ambivalent. This possibility is further underscored in the powerful last line by the oxymoronic neologism—"black-eloquent silence in the work" ("chernorechivoe molchanie v rabote")—that substitutes for the expected "eloquent" or even "grandiloquent" (*krasnorechivoe*). Substitution of the root "cherno-" (black/hard/heavy) for "krasno-" (red/beautiful), of course, refers back to the black earth's capacity for poetic creation expressed in the "thousand hills of ploughed up words." However, it may also be read as contrasting the "hard work" (*chernaia rabota*) accomplished by the earth, by the peasant's labor, and by the poet, to gratuitous Soviet rhetoric (*krasnorechie*).

Furthermore, stanza 2, which describes spring ploughing, defines the earth's "work" as "unarmed," for, as the archaic verb (*zizhdit'sia*) suggests, that work is in, or of, or created by, the earth, and as such is self-sufficient. It is represented by another neologism—a "thousand hills of ploughed-up words/speech" (*tysiachekholmiia molvy*)—and hence requires no extra protection. The neologisms—*pereuvazhena, perecherna, tysiachekholmiia molvy,* and *provorot,* and the oxymoronic *chernorechivoe molchanie*—may thus be read as the realization of the earth's work—the "thousand hills of words . . . ,"—while the archaic verb to build, create, found (*zizhdit'sia*) emphasizes the historical and metaphysical ontology of the creative process. The "black earth," apostrophized in the poem's last lines, is transmuted into the "black-eloquent silence" of poetry, the mysterious internal creative process that here implies a solemn rejection of official Soviet grandiloquence (*krasnorechie*).

The other fundamental characteristic of the earth—its implacable, inexorable nature—is suggested in stanzas 3 and 4 in conjunction with the poet's gradual inscription of himself into his medium. Conversational idiom and direct dialogue establish an immediate bond between the poet and the earth.

In no. 312, "Stanzas," an autobiographical cycle of eight poems recapitulating the poet's life in the 1930s, the final "Stanza" sums up the speaker's state of mind and projects his future as intimately linked with the earth. The poet defines his voice by claiming the earth itself will be his "weapon," and thus illuminates two major attributes of the earth—its "unarmed" and its inexorable nature.

> And after I get my breath back, in my voice
> The earth will resound—my final weapon—
> The dry moistness of the black earth.
> (no. 312, no. 8, May–June 1935)

In "Black Earth" Mandelstam associates the steadfast nature of the earth with the eternal creative process. He first introduces highly colloquial diction in stanza 3, using words such as *prorukha* and *obukh* (a blunder and a butt) and the phrase "*Kak v nogi ei ne bukhai*" (You can't plead with it, or fall at its feet) to indicate the inexorable power of the earth. He then compares it to musical instruments that irritate rather than soothe the ear, that "alert your hearing." This stanza recalls "To some winter is arrack," in which the poet's ear is alerted by the "cruel imperatives of the stars."[13]

Finally, in the concluding stanza the speaker addresses the earth directly, recalling the self-reflexive dialogue in *Journey to Armenia* where the poet first began to recognize his imperative: the "feeling for the fullness of life characteristic of the Armenian people . . . kept repeating to me: now stay awake, don't fear your own age, don't be coy." In this poem, his greetings to the earth are simultaneously self-exhortation: "Well, hello there, black earth, be brave, keep your eyes open / There's black-eloquent silence in [your] work." An analogy between the poet and the dual nature of the earth is thus drawn. Like the earth the poet both preserves and creates, and like the earth the poet's imperative is demanding and implacable.

Mandelstam's paean, then, is directed toward the organic creative process inscribed in the cyclical silent work of the earth readying itself for "April's turning of the soil" ("aprel'skii provorot"), which in turn is associated with the aesthetic and metaphysical impulses to creation implied in the traditional imagery of spring, growth, and resurrection, as well as in philosophical, indeed political, images of freedom, expressed as: "Moist clods of *my* earth and freedom." In addition, Mandelstam's poetic imperative so forcefully depicted in *1921–1925* in his adherence to "the stars" and reiterated in *Journey to Armenia* through the "verb on horseback," is subtly inscribed here in the earth through the imagery of horses' withers and grooming expressed in stanza 1: "all in peak condition, / All in the little withers, all clean air and grooming" ("vse *v khole, khol*khi, prizor"), and phonically associated with "freedom" ("*vol*ia") in stanza 1 and the "thousand hills of words" ("tysiache*khol*miia *mol*vy") in stanza 2. This hymn to the "black earth and its "black-eloquent silence" must thus be read as a reaffirmation of his poetic imperative, his aesthetic principle of unity and synthesis, preservation and promise, as well as an assertion of poetic freedom, a statement of defiance before time and the age.

Death and Exorcism

Baines[14] has shown that "Black Earth" was the master poem of a cycle (nos. 300–307) in which the poet's ambivalent vision associated the motif of the earth with self-affirmation or promise on the one hand, but emphasized the theme of death on the other.

Poem no. 305, "I must live, though I've already died twice" ("Ia dolzhen zhit', khotia ia dvazhdy umer") begins with an affirmation of the poet's autobiographical imperative to continue living and writing poetry. It affirms life by reiterating the imagery of the "silent" steppe and its motifs of renewal and faith in the creative process.

On the other hand, in no. 306, "Yes, I am lying in the earth, moving my lips" ("Da, ia lezhu v zemle . . ."), a self-reflexive epitaph, the speaker's posthumous voice predicts immortality for his verse, if not for himself: "But what I am about to say *will be learned* by every schoolboy." This poem blends the theme of the poet's imperative with the Acmeist ideal of the poet's role as teacher of mankind from "On the Nature of the Word."

In contrast to the thematics of affirmation, the *First Voronezh Notebook* also contains anguished appeals for release (no. 301, "Let me go, Voronezh . . ." ["Pusti menia, Voronezh . . ."]), images of death as terrifyingly real and imminent (no. 304, "I live in a proper kitchen garden" ["Ia zhivu na vazhnykh ogorodakh"]), and even a mystical nightmare recollecting the horrors of Mandelstam's five-day Calvary, his exile journey to Cherdyn (no. 313, "The Day was Five-headed" ["Den' stoial na piati golovakh," April-June 1935]).

"Let me go, Voronezh" is a kind of exorcism,—a single quatrain through which the poet attempts to divine his fate by conjuring up insidious puns on the name Voronezh: *voron* (raven), *nozh* (knife). The verbs are especially keen: *uronish'*, *provoronish'*, *vyronish'*, *vernesh'* (you will drop, waste, let drop, return).

"The Day was Five-headed," also verges on mystical exorcism, for its theme of madness provides the speaker's only hope of escape. Madness allows the poet-speaker to envision himself as the semi-mythical hero, Chapaev, who, in the concluding stanza, "dies, and jumps on his horse."[15] This self-reminiscence recalls, indeed enacts, Mandelstam's Armenian imperative. Madness also reemerges as a positive theme in no. 380, "Maybe this is the beginning of madness" ("Mozhet byt' eto tochka bezumiia") from the last *Voronezh Notebook*.

By July 1935 another significant motif appears in conjunction with the theme of death: the poet's tragic vision of shared identity with the nameless masses, common soldiers suffering an aerial death. However, this is fully developed only two years later in Mandelstam's last major poetic cycle, "Verses on the Unknown Soldier," wherein he attempts an "answer" to the unanswerable question concluding no. 320, "Not like a floury white butterfly" ("Ne muchnistoi babochkoiu beloi"). Here, the poet-speaker juxtaposes his personal desire for a meaningful, poetic death with the loss of individual identity in the mass procession into oblivion:

. . . I want this thinking body
To be turned into a street, a nation—
This vertebral, charred body,
Conscious of its own length.

Comrades—the latest recruits—marched
To work in the hardened sky,
The infantry passed silently
Exclamations of rifles on their shoulders.

And thousands of guns aimed at the air—
Were they hazel eyes or blue—
They marched in confusion—people, people, people—
Who will continue on for them?

(no. 320, July 1935)

Second Voronezh Notebook

This apocalyptic vision was followed by silence until December
1936, when the *Second Voronezh Notebook* began to take shape. At least
in part stimulated by contradictory feelings of apprehension and defiance as well as guilt and remorse with respect to Stalin,[16] two major
themes dominate this *Notebook*: the joy of creation and the haunting
image of Stalin.

Poem no. 342, "Birth of a Smile" ("Rozhdenie ulybki"), the second
poem of the *Second Notebook,* continues the imagery and thematics of
creation presented in "The Octets," namely, the poet's joy in the presence of the phenomenon of creation; the metaphorical association of
poetic creation and the metaphysical realm; and the motifs of intuition,
spontaneity, and teleology so essential to the poet's capacity to recognize, and hence realize, the miracle of creation. Most important, perhaps, in "Birth of a Smile," as in "The Octets," the poetic process itself
demonstrates teleological design. The poet's vision of the origins of
poetic creation depicted through the organic, scientific, poetic, and
teleological unfolding of the miracle of creation, along with his faith
in cosmic unity and continuity bearing the promise of the future, are
realized once again in the image of "the child," here expressed in the
metonymical "smile" and in the emergence of the lost continent of
Atlantis as it "strikes the eyes."

When a child begins to smile,
Parted lips reveal sorrow and sweetness,
The corners of his smile, unlaughing,
Recede into the ocean's anarchy.

Feeling so inexplicably fine,
The corners of his mouth play in the glory—
And a rainbow seam is already being stitched
Into the eternal cognition of the real.

The continent on its paws rears up from the deep—
The helix of the mouth looms up, approaches—
One moment of Atlantis strikes your eyes:
Realization of the real in the miracles of the universe.

Space has lost its color and taste
The continent has risen, spine and arc,
The helix snail crawls out, the smile bursts forth,
As their two ends are tied by a rainbow
And the moment of Atlantis strikes both eyes.
        (no. 342, 9 December 1936–11 January 1937)

Furthermore, like Mandelstam's hymn to "the black earth," his paean to "the child's smile," is gradually metamorphosed into praise of the miracle of creation. His metaphysical vision of the birth of Atlantis is realized through an intricate combination of linguistic and semantic elements—simple diction of sentimental emotion interacts with physical and metaphysical terminology.

For example, the theme of unity and continuity between the physical and metaphysical worlds is expressed, as in most of Mandelstam's later verse, through phonosemantic metamorphoses of organic and poetic images of creation. Establishing equivalence through phonic relationships as well as through the imagery of the circular form or endless spiral—between the spiral-shaped snail shell or helix/cochlea (*ulit*ka) and the smile (*ulyb*ka), whose corners meet and merge in the metaphysical, in "Ocean's anarchy/chaos"—suggests the possibility of analogy, and hence unity, of even the most antithetical phenomena, reinforcing Mandelstam's view of the synthetic nature and even purpose of the creative process.

The poet-speaker's witnessing of the process of creation in this poem thus testifies to Mandelstam's teleological vision, to the phenomenon of "the realization of the real" ("iavlen'ia iavnogo"), the coming into being of the miracle of life (*v chislo chudes vselen'ia*). Mandelstam's mythopoetic covenant—the idea of eternal cognition or recognition of the real—recalls "Tristia": "And only the moment of recognition is sweet." It reemerges as affirmation of faith in the promise of "synthesis" defined in his earliest verse, later in "Word and Culture," where the poet-synthesizer is identified with Verlaine, and subsequently in *Conversation about Dante,* in his more theoretical pronouncement that the process of "transmutation and hybridization" is the basis of the poetic process.

Almost simultaneously with "Birth of a Smile," Mandelstam composed no. 330, "Inside a mountain Idles an Idol" ("Vnutri gory bezdeistvuet kumir," 10–26 December 1936) which both in its malicious tone and in its extremely negative physiological characterization of Stalin recalls the "Epigram." Indeed, no. 330 records a nightmare in which the poet-speaker envisions Stalin—the repulsive "idol"—as once also having had a childhood, as once also subject to a covenant, but now reduced to "laboring to remember his own human countenance." Adhering structurally to one of the unique features of Mandelstam's later poetry—the admission of an odd number of lines—this poem resembles "Birth of a Smile." The final stanzas each contain an "extra" line, thereby creating extraordinarily powerful conclusions. Compare "And the flash of Atlantis strikes both eyes" with "And he labors to remember his own human countenance."

The "Ode to Stalin"

One more reference to Stalin appears in early 1937. Among other passages desperately crying out for help, Mandelstam wrote the following in a letter to Korney Chukovsky: "There is now only one person in the whole world to whom I can and must turn. . . ."[17]

When Mandelstam finally sat down to compose his "Ode to Stalin" on 12 January 1937,[18] both sets of images intersected, bonding with the extraordinary "impulse" behind the conjunction of human, spiritual, and ideological polarities marking the poet's larger theme—the ambiguous relationship between the powerful and the weak, oppressor and victim, tyrant and subject, father and son, even creator and creation—that informs the "Ode" and the twenty or so poems of this period motivated by its composition, the "Ode" cycle.

In trying to place the "Ode to Stalin" in the "ideological and myth-ological framework of Mandelstam's writings," Freidin notes that it was composed as the poet's term of exile was coming to an end, when he was increasingly apprehensive about his future, and thus decided to try to buy his freedom "by paying Stalin in poetic kind." Nevertheless, he perceives the "Ode" as much more than "doggerel," even as "a mag-nificent paean." He interprets it as a masterpiece that allowed the poet to fulfill the artist's role of *imitatio Christi* identified in his early unfin-ished essay, "Pushkin and Scriabin": "the scenario [Mandelstam] out-lined for himself in the 'Ode' in such gruesome detail (stanza 5) did include, as in the case of Christ, humiliation, suffering and death. And yet, whatever other reasons for the composition of the poem, he clearly sought in it a "catharsis, redemption," as he put it [in "Pushkin and Scriabin"] not through but "in art": justification of his fate in Christ's likeness and image. . . . As a magic spell it proved to be quite effective."[19]

Equally significant, perhaps, Mandelstam's ultimate reaffirmation of his synthetic principle, his mythopoetic yearning for freedom through the union of opposing principles, may also have influenced his incred-ible "transmutation and hybridization" of the themes of creation and Stalin, first in the "Ode," and subsequently in the verse it generated. This aesthetic principle may also at least partly explain his introduction of Christian symbolism into the "Ode" as the supreme expression of faith in the ideals of unity and continuity. Begun both as an attempt to expiate his own guilt by inscribing himself in the role of the one who takes mankind's guilt unto himself, and ultimately as an attempt to redeem the world through poetic creation, by inscribing himself in the role of savior (the one to be resurrected in order to resurrect man-kind), the poet's endeavor to invoke Stalin as father and creator (not tormentor) bound to the poet as Son and Messiah—bearer of truth to posterity (not victim), once again shaped his work into a mystical-poetic exorcism.[20] Indeed, the association of his own attributes with those of his tormentor—the mystical bonding of their given names through the word, "axis" (*os'*)—suggests their shared identity and des-tiny, offering Mandelstam mystical protection against both moral deg-radation and oblivion. The "Ode," then, and the cycle of poems generated by it, seem to have refocused his poetic impulses by exorcis-ing Stalin's power over him.

The twenty-four poems comprising the "Ode" cycle, the remainder of the *Second Voronezh Notebook,* cover a broad thematic and tonal spectrum, some emphasizing Mandelstam's allegiance to the age, others his sense of defiance, others being politically neutral. For instance, in the "twin poems"[21] dated 12–18 January, nos. 346–347, "Precious Yeast of the World" ("Drozhzhi mira dorogie"), and no. 348, "A little demon in wet fur crept in" ("Vlez besenok v mokroi sherstke"), Mandelstam hints that something "not his own," something "as if from the side," caused all his troubles—something "mocking and knocking [him] off his true axis"—forcing him to substitute the extraneous for his true task. Nadezhda Mandelstam, presenting the canonical view that Mandelstam did not willingly write the "Ode,"[22] refers to this cycle as "free poems" and suggests that the "Ode" was at cross purposes with his verse.

The major themes of this cycle range from apologetics for the "Ode" (no. 348, "A little demon . . .") to the theme of tragedy and martyrdom (no. 364, "Like Rembrandt, martyr of chiaroscuro" ["Kak svetoteni muchenik Rembrandt"]); from exaltation of humankind (no. 352: "Do not compare: the living are incomparable" ["Ne sravnivai: zhivushchii nesravnim"]) and love of life (the last stanza of no. 370, "I'm down in a lion's ditch" ["Ia v l'vinyi rov . . ."]) to reaffirmation of the "people's need" for poetry (no. 355) and reaffirmation of his own poetic imperative (no. 365, "I sing when my throat is moist"). This cycle also treats the theme of "reality" as an absolute which along with "breathing" must be acknowledged as worthy of love and poetry, (no. 359, "I love frosty breath . . . and reality is reality!" ["Liubliu moroznoe dykhan'e," 24 January 1937]), as well as the other side of "reality," the terrible pain of homelessness and isolation (no. 360, "Where can I go, now it's January?" ["Kuda mne det'sia v etom Ianvare?"]) with its poignantly evocative, wishful conclusion: "If I could have a real conversation—a reader, an adviser, a doctor! / Someone to talk to on the jagged stairs!" In addition, as Freidin points out, this cycle includes poems maintaining an obsequious attitude toward Stalin, for example, metonyms "pulled out of a propaganda poster" in no. 371 "Sleep defends my Don drowsiness" ("Oboroniaet son moiu donskuiu son'"), or the image of the poet rushing into the Kremlin to avow his guilt—"my head heavy with guilt"—before the leader in no. 361. Hence, whether they develop, negate, or reinforce its elements, the poems of this cycle are all loosely interconnected through the "Ode."

Two extraordinary examples, written on the same day, 8 February 1937 and linked through the imagery of "axis," singing, and poetic imperative, are no. 367, "Armed with the vision of narrow wasps"

("Vooruzhennyi zren'em uzkikh os"), and no. 365, "I sing when my throat is damp . . ." ("Poiu kogda gortan' syra . . .").

While in the "Ode," the poet-speaker presents himself as seeking an "axis of likeness" (*skhodstva os'*) with Stalin (stanza 5), and Stalin is presented as having "shifted the world's axis" (stanza 1), in no. 367, the poet-speaker acknowledges the failure of his creative powers—"I do not sing"—as a result of his inability to "hear the earth's axis." Nevertheless, he establishes his faith in the power of poetry through verbal magic or incantation. He yearns for that day in the future when he shall again "hear the earth's axis" (*os' zemnuiu*). By expressing his yearning in the form of a wish-fantasy, the poet recalls not only the magical flight of fancy in no. 202, the wish to "whistle through life eating nutpie," or the exorcisms of the "Black earth" cycle, but the incantatory dream-fantasy of "Fourth Prose," his would-be journey to Armenia, which when finally realized led to the return of his poetic voice. In no. 367, the poet-speaker's wish to avert "sleep and death," so that "some day" he might again "hear the earth's axis," is but another form of incantation invoking the return of his poetic voice—to "hear" his poetic imperative so as to challenge time through "creative cognition."[23] Indeed, as we have already noted in discussing the Armenian cycle and the *First Voronezh Notebook,* Mandelstam had to "hear" the imperative of "the earth." Vision alone, no matter how penetrating, was inadequate. His yearning to renew his relationship to the earth— to "hear the earth's axis"—is thus tantamount to invoking the return of his poetic imperative.

> Armed with the sight of narrow wasps
> Sucking at the earth's axis, the earth's axis,
> I reexperience everything I've had to meet,
> I remember it by heart, and in vain.
>
> I do not draw, nor do I sing,
> Nor move my dark-voiced bow.
> I only make a little hole in life and enjoy
> Envying the powerful cunning wasps.
>
> Oh, if only some day the sting of the air and
> The summer warmth could make me—
> Passing by sleep and death—
> Hear the earth's axis, the earth's axis. . . .
>
> (no. 367, 8 February 1937)

Mandelstam's poetic imperative is also the subject of no. 365, which uses imagery directly recalling the theme of its reaffirmation in *Journey to Armenia*. Mandelstam projects himself into the likeness of the Caucasian horsemen whose proud task it is to honorably and joyously escort betrothed couples through the dangers of the mountains, singing them "sinless" to their wedding. He thus proclaims his song "selfless" and "pure," his "conscience"—free and clear.

Furthermore, in this poem Mandelstam may be asking after the "health" of the entire Black Sea region—Colchis, the legendary land of the Golden Fleece, of his beloved Crimea, Georgia, and Armenia. Indeed, this poem would seem to expand upon his Armenian covenant. Even the phrase "and my head's deaf" (*golova glukha*) is best interpreted by recalling the paragraphs on the origins of language, the development of concepts and of legend in *Journey to Armenia*. The declaration "it is no longer me singing" implies that his imperative has taken over, clarifying the image "my hearing's sheathed in the mountain" and "my head's deaf," for his "song" now comes from within. "Creative cognition" reigns, and the poet's song emerges natural and pure. The couplet introduced between the two lengthier stanzas provides the only justification Mandelstam sought for his verse; hence, no. 365 may serve as his song of redemption:

> I sing when my throat is damp and my soul dry,
> My vision properly moist, and my conscience clear.
> Is wine healthy? Are furs?
> Or the blood stirring within all that is Colchis?
> But my chest grows shy, silent without language:
> It's no longer me singing—it's my breath—
> My hearing's sheathed in the mountain and my head's deaf.
>
> A selfless song is its own praise.
> A comfort for friends, pitch for enemies.
>
> A single-eyed song growing out of moss,
> A single-voiced gift of hunting life,
> Which they sing on horseback and in the heights,
> Breathing freely and openly,
> Honorably and sternly caring only to transport
> The young couple sinless to their wedding.
>
> (no. 365, 8 February 1937)

"Verses on the Unknown Soldier"

In February–March 1937 Mandelstam began his last, and possibly most complex poetic cycle, no. 362, "Verses on the Unknown Soldier" ("Stikhi o neizvestnom soldate").[24] This dense and lengthy master-piece, in effect the poet's requiem for mankind, marked the end of the "Ode" cycle and the beginning of the *Third Voronezh Notebook*. As the "Unknown Solder" evolved over a period of three months, shorter lyrics emerged simultaneously, forming the remainder of that collection. Poems no. 380, "Maybe this is a sign of madness" (15 March 1937), and no. 394, "Toward the Empty Earth . . ." (4 May 1937), treating the theme of woman's compassion and love as source of immortality, are of particular note.

"Verses on the Unknown Soldier," however, dominates the *Third Notebook*. Its thematics and the lack of a definitive text allow for more than one interpretation. Indeed, it was not until the end of May that at least one definitive text was recorded, but, according to Nadezhda Yakovlevna, Mandelstam took drafts with him to Samatikha, the writers' rest home outside of Moscow, where he was arrested never to return. Hence, an authorized text does not exist.[25]

Although the basic motifs and narrative structure of Mandelstam's cycle are discernible, its imagery is often dependent on subtextual references. Unfortunately, we can attempt only a brief summary here.

The "Unknown Soldier" consists of eight parts of unequal lengths, united by a common metrical pattern—anapestic trimeter—and, according to Levin, through analogy with the musical form of the "oratorio." Part 1, fulfilling the function of the exposition, enunciates the poet's major themes: the cosmos, eternal moral testimony, and death. They are expressed through the voice of the poet-speaker, who invokes the "air" as a "witness" (1.1). However, even "judge and witness" are subject to the "watchful stars," whose ultimate judgment (1.2) is linked to their metaphysical power which recalls the poet's adherence to the "cruel imperatives of the stars" in *1921–1925* (no. 127, "To some winter is arrack").[26] The theme of man's inevitable conflict with the divine forces of the universe and the lyrical reiteration of the ultimate questions of life and death raised here invoke traditions of Russian philosophical or meditative poetry going back at least to Lomonosov's "Meditations" and to Mandelstam's own meditative verse of *1921–1925*.[27]

Not only are the themes of death, war and destruction, and suffering, presented (1.4), but their calamitous continuation, like rain, is forecast (1.3). Nevertheless, while their victim, "the unknown soldier," has already been "put in his grave," the poet-speaker assumes his posthumous voice (1.5–6). The implication that the poet-persona speaks in the voice of the "unknown soldier" (1.5) is made explicit in his assertion that he will give a "strict report for Lermontov" about "how the grave teaches the stoop-shouldered" (1.6),[28] that is, he will challenge Lermontov's sanguine assumptions about cosmic harmony. On the other hand, the statement that the "aerial pit leads him on" establishes the poet's sense of his "right" to speak for mankind, since death, the source of his renewed imperative, inspires him to continue to write poetry in the form of this requiem. The Lermontov subtext is highly significant here, for as Kiril Taranovsky[29] has pointed out, Mandelstam's premonition of impending cataclysm opposes Lermontov's sense of cosmic harmony as presented in *Demon*:

> Through the airy ocean
> Without rudder or sail,
> Harmonious chorus of luminaries
> Calmly float in the mist.

Mandelstam's own self-reminiscences, namely, to *Tristia* and the swallow image recalling the Persephone myth, are also extremely significant.[30] In appeals to the "sickly swallow / Who has forgotten how to fly," Mandelstam's speaker recalls the vicarious anguish of the poet-persona in no. 113, "I have forgotten the word . . . ," as he follows the journey of the "blind swallow" ("the word") down into the underworld. Allusions to *Tristia* universalize his earlier vision of dying Russian culture, associating the poet in this instance not only with the shared destiny of his age, but with the common destiny of mankind. In asking the swallow to be his Muse, to teach him to master "this aerial grave," he invokes not only Russia but the entire universe as the subject of his requiem. Furthermore, the persona's experience of poetic pain as well as poetic rapture in "I have forgotten the word . . ." is reintroduced here through the themes of memory and death, always linked in Mandelstam's work with poetry or song. Death is again accompanied by the "night chorus" of "I have forgotten the word," the antithesis of Lermontov's "Harmonious chorus of luminaries."

Thus, Mandelstam's vision of the imminence of death determines the focus of "Verses on the Unknown Soldier." The voice of the poet as "witness," subject only to the "watchful stars," is juxtaposed to, as well as, merged with, the posthumous voice of human destiny—that of the common man, the "unknown soldier," speaking from his "aerial grave" (1.4–5). Death grants the poet the right to speak both "with his age" and "for everyone," eliminating the fear and ambivalence of the earlier collections.

Part 1.
Let *this* air be witness—
His long-range heart—
Omnivorous and active in the dug-outs too—
An ocean, matter minus a window.

How watchful *these* stars:
Why must they watch everything?
In judgement of judge and witness,
In the ocean, matter minus a window.

The rain, the unfriendly sower,
His nameless manna,
Remembers how a forest of little crosses mark
The ocean or the battle salient.

Cold, sickly people will kill,
Will suffer cold and hunger,
And an *unknown soldier*
Has been put in his famous grave.

Teach me, sickly swallow
Who has forgotten how to fly,
How I am to master this aerial grave
Without rudder or wing?

And for Lermontov, Mikhail,
I shall give you a strict report
How the grave teaches the stooping
And the aerial pit leads him on.
                    (3 March 1937, Voronezh; my italics)

The brief seven lines of part 2 speak of the evil nature of the contemporary world and hence its threat to Mankind. Parts 2, 5, and 6 are as

variations on the main themes, while part 7, in reiterating the themes
of part 1, acts as a kind of reprise:

> Part 2.
> Like grapes rustling on the vine
> *These* worlds threaten us,
> They hang like stolen towns,
> Like golden slips of the tongue, bits of false evidence—
> Berries of poisonous cold—
> The tents of tensile constellations—
> The golden worlds of constellations.

The mystical, mythical, and numerological message of part 3 seems
to be an effort to assure eternal memory and hope in the future, after
the Apocalypse, through a mystical Coming. The message of prophecy,
"I am the new—the world will be illumined by me," offers the Gospel
of John to the "reader in posterity":

> Part 3.
> Through the decimalized ether,
> The light of velocities ground into a ray
> Begins a number made transparent
> By the lucid pain and mol of zeroes.
>
> But beyond the field of fields a new field
> Is flying like a triangular crane—
> The message flies on a path of light-dust—
> And yesterday's battle creates light.
>
> The message flies on path of light-dust—
> I'm not Leipzig, not Waterloo,
> I'm not the Battle of Nations. *I am the new—*
> *The world will be illumined by me.*
>
> In the depths of his black-marble shell
> The spark of Austerlitz has gone out—
> The Mediterranean swallow screws up its eyes,
> the pestilential sands of Egypt congeal.

Part 4, stanza 1, seems to inscribe the voice of the poet—"the ray
is standing on my retina"—into the voice of prophecy expressed in part
3—the bearer of "light" to the new world after the Apocalypse. Part

4, stanza 2, a clear statement of Mandelstam's pacifism in the face of
senseless human slaughter, was arranged as the second stanza of the
entire poem and sent as a peace offering to *Znamya* on 11 March 1937,
in a last abortive effort to get something published.

Part 4, stanza 3, both echoes and enacts the line, "We will die like
footsoldiers," Mandelstam's premonition voiced in no. 260, "Midnight
in Moscow," and attempts to answer the ultimate question posed in
no. 320, "Not like a floury white butterfly": "*Who* will continue on
for [the millions marching into death and oblivion]?" The answer offered here is the poet, in the name of the "unknown soldier," the posthumous spokesman for mankind. Hence, parts 3 and 4 continue and
develop the themes of part 1:

> Part 4.
> An Arabian mash, a jumble,
> The light of velocities ground into a ray—
> And with its scythe-bearing feet
> *The ray is standing on my retina.*
>
> Millions of cannon fodder
> Have tramped the path in the emptiness,
> Good night, all the best to them,
> On behalf of the earthen fortifications.
>
> Incorruptible trench sky,
> Sky of great wholesale deaths,
> After you—away from you—O totality of sky
> *I rush with my lips in the darkness.*
>
> Past craters, embankments, and screes,
> Through which he hazily dawdled,
> The dour, pockmarked and servile genius
> Of the shattered graves.

Part 5 returns once again to "Midnight in Moscow," repeating the
line "We will die like footsoldiers" from the perspective of the "witness," and to "I have forgotten the word . . .," invoking the "night
chorus" to sing for the world's dead and crippled. The poet enters an
ironic plea to cease the destruction of the human race that has created
an Age of Cripples:

Part 5.
The infantry dies well,
The night chorus sings well
Over Schweik's flattened smile,
And over Don Quixote's bird-like spear
And over the bird's metatarsus.
And the cripple makes friends with man;
Both of them will be found work.
And the family of wooden crutches
Knocks on the outskirts of the age—
Hey, the earth's globe is a comradely union.

Part 6 appears to be a statement of the poet's wonderment at the human condition, a hymn to "creative cognition." The metonymy of the human skull refers not only to Shakespeare—the acme of human creative power—but to Mandelstam's own dream-vision in *Journey to Armenia*: "How I longed to return to the place where human skulls are equally beautiful at work or in the grave." The human skull, as the poet's microcosm of the universe, may thus offer a ray of hope for the future after the apocalypse:

Part 6.
Is it because the skull must develop
Into an entire forehead from temple to temple
That troops cannot help pouring
Into its precious eye-sockets?
The skull develops out of life
Into an entire forehead from temple to temple,
It teases itself with the cleanness of its seams,
It clarifies itself as an understanding cupola,
It froths with thought, it dreams of itself—
Chalice of chalices, fatherland of fatherlands—
Bonnet sewn with a seam of stars—
Cap of happiness—father of Shakespeare.

Part 7, in reiterating the themes of part 1, strengthens the idea of the poet as under a spell, and optimistically questions the stars about divining man's future. Especially interesting is part 7, stanza 2—the poet's rejoicing in the glorious struggle for "subsistence air" associated with "excess." This recalls his defiant declaration in "Fourth Prose" that the basis of genuine—"nonofficial"—art is "stolen air." In that work not only did he find the "doughnut's value resides in the hole," but he praised Brussel's lace for its "major components . . . air, perforations, and truancy." Indeed, part 7 presents what the poet knows, sees, and intuits, as well as what he hopes to divine. As in his earlier collections, he prophesies redemption through art by suggesting the possibility of divining the future and defying "official" formulas:

Part 7.
The clarity of the ash and perspicacity of the sycamore
Rush into their house with a touch of redness,
As if casting a spell semi-consciously
On both skies with their dim fires.

Only what is excess is allied with us,
Before us is not a fall, but a sounding,
And the fight for our *subsistence air*
Is a glory without peer.

And glutting my mind
With semi-conscious existence,
Do I drink this broth without choice,
Do I consume my head under fire!

Has the tare been drawn up
For enchantment in empty space,
So that white stars can race back into their house
With a touch of redness!—

Can you hear, O stepmother of the starry camp,—
O night, what will be now and in the future?

And finally, in part 8, which Levin terms the coda, the poet emerges in the lineup of the dead—among those awaiting resurrection and the overcoming of anonymity. As Ronen points out, the major impulse behind this poem is Mandelstam's "profound effort to overcome the anonymity of 'wholesale death.'"[31] He terms this conclusion a perfect example of what Segal called "ambivalent antithesis,"[32] for although Mandelstam prophesies the apocalypse, he also expresses faith in mankind's ultimate moral redemption—a collective resurrection guaranteed by the poetic word and reiterated here in the evocation of immortality: "the aortas [of the dead] are filled with blood," the living

poet-speaker "whispers through [his] blood-drained lips." Furthermore, as Levin indicates, the poet-speaker, concretized and individualized, appears in the subjective authorial role as well as in the role of
object—as a persona, ordinary and thus central, assuming the role of
the one who has found the "unknown soldier's" gift of speech. The
poet—identified by Mandelstam's birthdate—is at the very center of
the human-cosmic tragedy: "the centuries surround me with fire."
Hence, the universality of this requiem:

> Part 8.
> Aortas fill with blood
> And a quiet whisper resounds through the ranks:
> "I was born in ninety-four,
> I was born in ninety-two . . ."
> And amidst the mob and the mass,
> Squeezing my outworn birthdate in my fist,
> I whisper through my blood-drained lips:
> "I was born the night of the 2nd-3rd
> Of January in the ninety-first
> Unreliable year, and the centuries
> Surround me with fire."
>   (part 8, February–March 1937, Voronezh)

Mandelstam's magnificent farewell poem, no. 394, "Toward the
empty earth" ("K pustoi zemle nevol'no pripadaia"), is no longer about
the "unknown soldiers" who marched into death and oblivion, but
about those whose "calling" is "To escort the dead and be first / To
greet the resurrected," a subtextual reference to the "blessed women"
of no. 118, "We shall gather again in Petersburg / To bury the
sun. . . ."[33] Begun as an impassioned tribute to Natasha Shtempel[34],
who along with Nadezhda Mandelstam miraculously managed to preserve the poet's Voronezh verse, it emerges as a fervent hymn to love,
beauty, and immortality. Particularly noteworthy is the way perma-
nence resounds in the echo of footsteps, in the repetition of nouns and
verbs of movement and accompaniment, and in the remarkable re-
creation of the continuity and discontinuity of time past, present, and
future. Presence and absence, prescience and loss, promise and sacrifice
are ascribed to the reality of the earth, to spring, and to life, as well
as to premonitions of promise and resurrection. The second half of this
poem—nearly impossible to render in English—reads approximately:

There are women kin to the damp earth,
In whose every step reverberates sobbing;
To escort the dead and be first
To greet the resurrected is their calling.
To demand caresses from them is criminal.
To part with them is beyond endurance.
An angel—today; a worm in the grave—tomorrow.
A mere outline—the day after that.
What had been her step—is unrecognizable.
Flowers are immortal. Heaven is whole.
And what will be—is but a promise.

                                        (no. 394, 4 May 1937)

Poetic justice alone can redeem Mandelstam's "sacrifice" to the power, joy, and truth of poetry. The poet's life and work may be perceived as a fulfilment of his poetic prescience: "People need poetry . . . to keep them awake forever." His last will and testament, his final collection containing both his requiem and hymn to humankind, offers as the poet's greatest gift the "promise" of poetic testimony to his "reader in posterity."

Notes and References

Chapter One

1. See *The Noise of Time: The Prose of Osip Mandelstam*, trans. Clarence Brown (San Francisco: North Point Press, 1986). All page references are to this translation with slight revisions or emendations. Italics are mine unless otherwise noted.

2. For more details see "The Myth of St. Petersburg" in chapter 3.

3. *Sobranie sochinenii*, ed. Gleb Struve and Boris Filippov, 4 vols., 2d ed. rev. (Washington, D.C.: Inter-Language Literary Associates, 1964–71; Paris: YMCA Press, 1981); hereafter cited in text the as *SS*. All numbers are given according to the numbering system of *SS*. Translations and italics are mine unless otherwise indicated.

4. For further biographical details see Clarence Brown, *Mandelstam* (Cambridge: Cambridge University Press, 1973).

5. *Mandelstam: The Complete Critical Prose and Letters*, trans. Jane G. Harris and Constance Link (Ann Arbor, Mich.: Ardis Publishers, 1979); hereafter cited in the text as *CPL*. All citations to Mandelstam's letters, essays, and prose refer to this text unless otherwise noted. Italics are mine unless otherwise noted.

6. See *SS*, 1:6–7, 8–9, 120.

7. See Steven Broyde, *Osip Mandelstam and His Age* (Cambridge, Mass.: Harvard University Press, 1975), chap. 3.

8. See "The Uses of Ambiguity" in chapter 3.

9. Nadezhda Mandelstam, *Hope Against Hope*, trans. Max Hayward (New York: Athenaeum, 1972), 112–13.

10. For more details see *SS*, 2:604–17; Nadezhda Mandelstam, *Hope Against Hope*, 178, Nadezhda Mandelstam, *Hope Abandoned*, trans. Max Hayward (New York: Athenaeum, 1974), 360.

11. See *CPL*, no. 64a, 326–27; *SS*, 2:477–80.

12. See Boris Eikhenbaum, "O Mandel'shtame (14 Marta 1933)" (On Mandelstam [14 March 1933]), *Den'poezii* (Poetry day) (Leningrad, 1967), 167–68; and Lidiia Ginzburg, "The Poetics of Osip Mandelstam," trans. Sona Hoisington, in *Twentieth Century Russian Literary Criticism*, ed. Victor Ehrlich (New Haven, Conn.: Yale University Press, 1974), 284–312. Both mention Mandelstam's last visit to Leningrad as a major cultural event.

13. For more biographical details, see Nadezhda Mandelstam, *Hope Against Hope* and *Hope Abandoned*.

14. Nadezhda Mandelstam, *Hope Against Hope*, esp. chaps. 15–24.

Chapter Two

1. On Russian symbolism, see Georgette Donchin, *The Influence of French Symbolism on Russian Poetry* (The Hague: Mouton, 1958); and Evelyn Bristol, "Idealism and Decadence in Russian Symbolist Poetry," *Slavic Review* 39, no. 2 (1980):269–80.

2. Marcel Raymond, *From Baudelaire to Surrealism* (New York: Wittenborn, Schultz, 1949).

3. Donchin, *Influence,* 92–93. For more information on Tyutchev, see Richard A. Gregg, *Fedor Tiutchev: The Evolution of a Poet* (New York: Columbia University Press, 1965); S. M. Solovev and E. L. Radlov, eds., "Poeziia F. I. Tiutcheva" (The Poetry of F. I. Tiutchev), in *Sobranie sochinenii Vladimira Sergeevicha Solov'eva* (Collected works of Vladimir Solovev) (St. Petersburg, 1911), 7:117–34; V. Briusov, "Legenda o Tiutcheve" (The legend of Tyutchev), *Novyi put'* (New way) 11 (1903): 16–30; D. Blagoi, *"Tiutchev, ego kritiki i chitateli"* (Tyutchev: his critics and readers), *Tiutchevskii sbornik* (Tyutchev studies) (Petrograd 1923), 63–105; Sarah Pratt, *The Semantics of Chaos in Tiutchev* (Munich: Otto Sagner, 1983).

4. Paul Verlaine, *Selected Poems,* trans. C. F. MacIntyre (Berkeley: University of California Press, 1970).

5. For another interpretation of this poem, see E. A. Toddes, "Mandel'shtam i Tiutchev," *IJSLP* 17 (1974):59–85.

6. See Anna Akhmatova, "Mandel'shtam (Listki iz dnevnika)" (Mandelstam [pages from a diary]), in Anna Akhmatova, *Sochineniia* ed G. P. Struve and B. A. Fillipov. Washington, D.C.: Inter-Language Literary Associates, 1968. Vol. 2. Further references are to *SSA. SS:A,* 2:168–87.

7. Nadezhda Mandelstam, *Hope Against Hope,* 262.

8. See Nikolay Gumilev, *Sobranie sochinenii* (Collected Works, vols. 1–4) ed. G. P. Struve and B. A. Fillipov. Washington, D.C.: "Kamkin," 1968. Vol. 4. Further references are to *SSG. SS:G4.*

9. Ibid., 4:309.

10. Peter Steiner, "Poem as Manifesto," *Russian Literature* 5 (1977): 129–56.

11. See Kiril Taranovsky, *Essays on Mandel'shtam* (Cambridge, Mass.: Harvard University Press, 1976), 18, for a definition of "subtext" and for examples of its usage. See Bibliography for works of Omry Ronen and examples of subtextual analysis.

12. *Osip Mandelstam's "Stone,"* trans. Robert Tracy (Princeton, N.J.: Princeton University Press, 1981).

13. See Raoul Eshelman, "Mandelstam and Mystification," *Wiener Slawistischer Almanach* 12 (1983):163–80, for further discussion of "subtext" or "intertextuality" in Mandelstam's early verse.

14. See "The Background" in chapter 6.

Chapter Three

1. For fine analyses of this poem, see Nils A. Nilsson, *Osip Mandelstam: Five Poems* (Stockholm, 1974), 47–68; and Broyde, *Osip Mandelstam, chap. 3.*

2. Il'ia G. Erenburg, *Portrety russkikh poetov* (Portraits of Russian poets) (1922; reprint, Munich: Wilhelm Fink Verlag, Centrifuga Russian Reprintings and Printings, 1972), 104.

3. For an interesting assessment of Mandelstam's "Hellenism," see Ginzburg, "Poetics," 290.

4. Victor Terras, "Classical Motifs in the Poetry of Mandel'shtam," *Slavic and East European Journal* 10, no. 3 (1966):251–67.

5. V. V. Gippius, *Pushkin i khristianstvo* (Pushkin and Christianity) (St. Petersburg, 1915).

6. Brown, *Mandelstam,* 273.

7. For details see Ginzburg, "Poetics." Marina Tsvetaeva, "Istoriia odnogo posviashcheniia" (History of a dedication), *Oxford Slavonic Papers* 11 (1964):112–36, viewed Mandelstam's duality as due to his being a "Petersburger and a Crimean."

8. Broyde, *Osip Mandelstam,* 62. See also his valuable discussion of this poem.

9. In the first edition of *Tristia,* "We will gather again . . ." contains the phrase "Soviet night"; in later editions it is changed to "January." For further comments, see Broyde, *Osip Mandelstam,* and Brown, *Mandelstam.*

10. For more details, see Broyde, *Osip Mandelstam,* 102.

11. Cited in Ginzburg, "Poetics," 294.

Chapter Four

1. Citations of Mandelstam's *Noise of Time* refer first to the Brown translation in *The Noise of Time* and second to *SS,* 2:45–108. Italics are mine unless otherwise noted.

2. Henri Bergson, *Introduction to Metaphysics,* trans. T. E. Hulme (Paris, 1913; New York, 1949), 8.

3. Alexander Pushkin, *Little Tragedies: Four Short Verse Dramas,* ed. and trans. E. M. Kayden (Antioch, 1965), 91–93.

4. For other treatments of this work see, among others, Brown, "The Prose of Mandelstam," in *The Noise of Time*; B. Filipoff, "Proza Mandel'-shtama," in *SS,* 2:i–xviii; Grigory Freidin, "The Whisper of History and the Noise of Time," *Russian Review* 37, no. 4 (1978):421–37; Dmitry Segal, "Voprosy poeticheskoi organizatsii semantiki v proze Mandel'shtama" (Problems of the poetic organization of semantics in Mandelstam's prose), in *Russian Poetics: Proceedings of the International Colloquium at the University of California at Los Angeles, September 22–26, 1975,* ed. Thomas Eekman and Dean S. Worth, UCLA Slavic Series no. 4 (Berkeley: University of California Press, 1983).

Chapter Five

1. See Nadezhda Mandelstam, *Hope Against Hope* and *Hope Abandoned*.

2. See A. Grigor'ev and I. Petrova, "O. Mandelstam: Materialy k bio-grafii" (Mandelstam: biographical materials), *Russian Literature* 15 (1984):1–28. This article cites Mandelstam's translations of verse and prose from 1922 to 1930 and also lists his internal reviews and introductions to books of translations of this period.

3. For superb detailed discussions of the latter two poems see Omry Ronen, *An Approach to Mandel'stam* (Jerusalem: Magnes Press, 1983); on no. 136 see an excellent analysis by Broyde, *Osip Mandelstam*; on no. 137 see also Jennifer Baines, "Mandel'shtam's 'Grifel'naia oda': A Commentary in Light of the Unfinished Drafts," *Oxford Slavonic Papers* 5 (1975):61–82; Dmitry Segal, "O nekotorykh aspektakh semanticheskoi struktury 'Grifel'noi ody'" (On some aspects of the semantic structures of "Slate Ode"), *Russian Literature* 2 (1972):49–102; Victor Terras, "'Grifel'naia oda' Mandel'shtama (Mandel-stam's "Slate Ode"), *Novyi zhurnal* (New Review) 92 (1968):163–71; Irina M. Semenko, "O chernovikakh 'Grifel'noi ody'" (On the drafts of "Slate Ode"), in *Poetika pozdnego Mandel'shtama* (Poetics of the late Mandelstam) (Rome: Carucci editore, 1986), 9–35.

4. See Gumilev, *SSG:4*.

5. See Omry Ronen, "A Beam upon the Axe," *Slavica Hierosolymitana* (Jerusalem) 1 (1977):159. Ronen states: "The Acmeist virtues of loyalty, man-liness, and self-sacrifice had never been expressed more poignantly than they were in the dialogue of Mandelstam and Akhmatova. Nor should it be for-gotten that, faithful to the tradition of that dialogue, Akhmatova responded to the call of [Mandelstam's 1931 poem 'Preserve My Speech'] in her famous wartime pledge 'And we shall preserve you, Russian speech, / The great Rus-sian word' ('Manliness,' February 1942, 176)."

6. See Iurii I. Levin's superb semantic analysis of this poem in "Razbor odnogo stikhotvoreniia Mandel'shtama" (Analysis of a poem by Mandelstam), in *Slavic Poetics: Essays in Honor of Kiril Taranovsky* (The Hague: Mouton, 1973), 267–76.

7. Ronen, *Slavica Hierosolymitana,* 167. Although Ronen suggests a connection with Gumilev, he does not develop it; see Ibid., 159.

8. See Ronen, *An Approach to Mandel'stam,* 276: "'Salt' is a traditional symbol of fidelity to an oath or covenant. . . . In M's poetry, it combines the meanings of 'unswerving loyalty' and 'sorrow.'" For another interpretation of this poem see A. Khan, "Zametki o semantike kontekstnykh pereklichek" (Notes on the semantics of contextual references), *Dissertationes Slavicae: Pub-licationes instituti philologiae russicae in universitate de Attila Jozsef Nominatae* (Hungary) 12 (1977):3–28.

9. The last stanza was added much later, in 1936. It is adapted here from Bernard Meares's translation. See *Osip Mandestam: 50 Poems* (New York: Persea Books, 1977), 57.

10. See Broyde, *Osip Mandelstam,* 118.

11. See note 3.

12. For other readings of this work see Brown, The Noise of Time; Charles Isenberg, "Associative chains in 'Egipetskaia marka,'" *Russian Literature* 5, no. 3 (1977):257–76; Daphne West, *The Egyptian Stamp* (Birmingham, England: Birmingham Slavonic Monographs, no. 10, 1980); Dmitry Segal, "Voprosy poeticheskoi organizatsii v proze" and "Literatura kak okhrannaia gramota," *Slavica Hierosolymitana* 5–6 (1981):151–244.

13. Nadezhda Mandelstam, *Hope Against Hope,* 178.

14. For more details on "Fourth Prose" see Harris, "The Impulse and the Text," *CPL,* 26–31.

Chapter Six

1. Citations to this text refer first to *SS,* 2:137–76, and second to *CPL,* 244–78. Italics are mine unless otherwise noted. For other discussions of this text see, Nadezhda Mandelstam, *Literaturnaia Armeniia* (Literary Armenia) 3 (1967):99–101; Gevork Emin, ibid., 82–83; Irina M. Semenko, "Osip Mandel'shtam. Zapisnye knizhki. Zametki" (Osip Mandelstam. Notebooks. Comments) *Voprosy literatury* (Problems of literature) 4 (1968):180–204; Henry Gifford, "Mandelstam and the *Journey,*" in *Mandelstam: Journey to Armenia,* trans. Sidney Monas (San Francisco: George F. Ritchie, 1979), 7–33.

2. Poetic freedom in "Fourth Prose" includes ethical, aesthetic, and political freedom. It is in this work that Mandelstam recognizes his Jewish consciousness as the moral imperative or impulse behind his poetic consciousness and associates his ideal image of the poet with his image of the *raznochinets,* outcast, and Jew. For more details see "The Impulse and the Text," in *CPL,* 27–31, 661–62.

3. Nadezhda Mandelstam, *Literaturnaia Armeniia* and *Hope against Hope.*

4. Ivan Ivanovich Shopen (1798–1870), a Frenchman who served as a government official in Russia, best known as an ethnographer and historian of the Caucasus. Mandelstam may have known his *Novye zametki na drevnyia istorija Kavkaza i ego obitatelei (New commentary on the ancient history of the Caucasus and its inhabitants (St. Petersburg, 1866).*

5. Nikolay Marr (1864–1934), a specialist in Caucasian archaeology and linguistics, whose "Japhetic theories" were presented in several works including "Osnovnye dostizheniia iaficheskoi teorii" (Basic achievements of the Japhetic theory) (Leningrad, 1935). Most important, Mandelstam seemed to adhere to Marr's view that Armenian was the original language of mankind.

6. Josef Strzygowski (1862–1941), art historian who believed that the Armenian church was the model for all Christian church architecture. See *Ursprung der Christlichen Kirchenkunst* (Leipzig, 1920), translated into English as *Origin of Christian Church Art* (Oxford, 1923). This supported Mandelstam's

idea that Armenia was the source of European or Mediterranean culture and civilization. In addition, Mandelstam's fantasy of being inside St. Peter's in Rome as he experienced his "first sensual encounter with an Armenian church" (chap. 7) literally echoes Strzygowski: "the Hripsimeh church . . . [which] type is the most singular which occurs on Armenian soil . . . has found no favor beyond the Armenia border, unless S. Peter's at Rome can be regarded as an example" (63). Here, Mandelstam's journey clearly corroborated his reading.

7. See Boris S. Kuzin, "Ob O. E. Mandel'shtame" (On Mandelstam), *Vestnik russkogo khristianskogo dvizheniia* (Herald of the Russian Christian Movement) (Paris), 3–4, no. 140 (1983):99–129. Kuzin's arrest during the publication of this work in 1933 forced the publishers to give him the pseudonym A. B. Zotov in the original text. See *SS, 2*:600.

8. What Mandelstam calls "tombstones" are actually "cross-stones" (*khatchkars* in Armenian), stone stele carved with Christian symbols, either to commemorate the dead or as markers for other purposes or to be embedded in church walls. Mandelstam's reference indicates either a lack of knowledge of this subject or disregard for the significance of these stele to support his own theme, not untypical of Mandelstam. I am much indebted to Nina Garsoian of Columbia University's Armenian Institute for sharing her knowledge of Armenian history and culture with me.

9. Published in Paris in 1899, this manifesto was written in defense of the post-impressionists' use of color and contrast, and hence, Delacroix.

10. For more details on Mandelstam's prose style, see Segal, "Voprosy poeticheskoi organizatsii semantiki v proze": "Mandelstam's prose is constructed on the principle of asymmetry. . . . Hence, the above-noted 'absence of organization' of Mandelstam's prose, its 'fragmentary nature,' its abundance of 'unnecessary,' 'accidental details, the absence of completion, of circularity.'" See also Segal, "Literatura kak okhrannaia gramota."

11. Although Segal, in "Voprosy" is referring mainly to Mandelstam's *Egyptian Stamp,* what he says applies equally to *Journey to Armenia*: "what Tynianov considered the material of poetry (semantic groups) became in Mandelstam's prose a constructive principle. The author's personal, everyday experience of existence in a particular historico-cultural situation connected with a given space and time serves as the material of his prose (as the dominant elements). Accordingly, Mandelstam's prose is, first of all, 'poetically organized' at the very lowest levels of expression (including the levels of phonetics and syntax) and second, overcoming the poetic personality has always endowed this prose with a very significant supplement: *the living voice, conversation, dialogue* with the reader."

12. Mandelstam kept notes of his trip. See Semenko, "Zapisnye knizhki."

13. For information on the debates over environmental determinism, see David Joravsky, *Soviet Marxism and Natural Science* (New York: Columbia Uni-

versity Press, 1961), and *The Lysenko Affair* (Cambridge, Mass.: Harvard University Press, 1970); Zh. Medvedev, *The Rise and Fall of T. D. Lysenko* (New York: Columbia University Press, 1969).

14. See *100 Armenian Tales and their Folkloristic Relevance,* ed. Susie Hoogasian-Villa (Detroit: Wayne State University Press, 1966); Leon Z. Surmelian, *Apples of Immortality: Folktales* (Berkeley: University of California Press, 1968).

15. Mandelstam's "Ararat sense" signifies his sense of freedom and independence as well as his spiritual and poetic covenant. It should be interpreted as "Armenian sense," not merely an attraction to Mt. Ararat, for the inhabitants of the kingdom flourishing between the Araxes and Upper Tigris rivers in the ninth–seventh centuries B.C. were known to the Assyro-Babylonians as Urartu and the Hebrews as Ararat. A Persian legend terms Ararat the cradle of the human race, while the Judeo-Christian Bible treats Ararat as the sacred land of the Covenant: Genesis 8:4.

16. See the original in Faustus de Byzance, in Victor Langlois, *Collection des historiens anciens et modernes de l'Armenie* (Paris, 1867), bk. 5, chap. 7.

17. Tsezar' Volpe, editor of *Zvezda* (Star), lost his job for allowing this legend to be included in the publication of *Journey to Armenia* in 1933. See Nadezhda Mandelstam, *Hope against Hope,* 410.

18. Anioush means place of the "forgotten ones" or "unpersons" in Armenian.

Chapter Seven

1. Jennifer Baines, *Mandelstam: The Later Poetry* (Cambridge: Cambridge University Press, 1976). Baines asserts in her preface her reason for following the order of Nadezhda Mandelstam's "own typescript of Mandelstam's poetry": "When Mandelstam arranged his poems into collections (whether they were actually published or not) he almost invariably placed them in the chronological order in which they were written down for the first time—an order which was not necessarily that of their composition in all cases. This order [is] clearly very deliberate. . . ." In my discussions of the *Moscow Notebooks* and *Voronezh Notebooks* I adhere to the Baines–N. Mandelstam order given in Baines, *Mandelstam,* 237–44, but follow the numbering system of *SS.* According to Baines, "Mandelstam said that [this poem] came first and 'awoke' [the Armenian poems]. . . . Its completion came only with the producing of the 'nut pie.'" The typescript dates no. 202 as the first poem of *Moscow Notebooks,* 5–7. See also Irina M. Semenko, "Rannie redaktsii i varianty tsikla 'Armeniia'" (Early versions and variants of the "Armenia" cycle), in *Poetika pozdnego Mandel'shtama* (Rome: Carruci Editore, 1986), 36–55.

2. Geoffrey H. Hartman, *The Unmediated Vision* (New York: Harcourt, Brace & World, 1966), 164, 172–73.

3. Baines, *Mandelstam,* 5–7.

4. See Iurii I. Levin, "Zametki o poezii Mandel'stama tridtsatykh godov, I" (Notes on Mandelstam's poetry of the thirties), *Slavica Hierosolymitana* 3 (1978):110–73, for more details on Mandelstam's poetic "I" and his "new poetic norms."

5. See M. L. Gasparov, "Russkii trekhudarnyi dol'nik XX veka" (The Russian three-stressed *dolnik* in the twentieth century), *Teoriia stikha* (Theory of verse) (Leningrad, 1968), 97–106, for a discussion on three different types of *dolniks* in Russian poetry of the twentieth century.

6. Ginzburg, "The Poetics of Mandelstam," 312.

7. The Armenian poems are dated variously from 16 October through November 1930. See Baines, *Mandelstam,* 237–44.

8. Nadezhda Mandelstam, *Hope Against Hope,* 232.

9. See Iurii I. Levin, "Razbor dvukh stikhotvorenii Mandelstama" (Analysis of two poems by Mandelstam), *Russian Literature* 2 (1972):37–49, for an analysis of no. 221.

10. For more details on the satirical poems of this period see chapter 8.

11. The name of a Moscow clothing factory that produced jackets especially popular with the intelligentsia of the 1930s.

12. Ronen, *An Approach to Mandel'stam,* 320.

13. See Omry Ronen, "Chetvertoe soslovie: Vierte Stand or Fourth Estate? (A Rejoinder)," *Slavica Hierosolymitana* 5–6 (1981):319–24.

14. See chapter 8.

15. Baines, *Mandelstam,* 237–44. An analysis based on yet another order is found in Clarence Brown, "Mandelstam's Notes Toward a Supreme Fiction," *Delos: A Journal of Transition* 1 (1968).

16. See in particular "Verses on the Unknown Soldier" in chapter 8.

Chapter Eight

1. For accounts of the famous Pasternak–Stalin telephone conversation about Mandelstam's fate see Nadezhda Mandelstam, *Hope Against Hope,* chap. 32; *Pamiat'* (Memory), vol. 4 (Paris: YMCA Press, 1980).

2. Ginzburg, "The Poetics of Mandelstam," 292.

3. *Vorenezh Notebooks,* ed. Victoria Shveitzer (Ann Arbor, Mich.: Ardis, 1980).

4. See Levin, "Zametki o poezii Mandel'schtama tridtsatykh godov, I." Among others, Levin has claimed that the difficulty of Mandelstam's language is an "antidote" to the meaninglessness and Aesopian jargon of official Soviet formulas. This, however, can only be partially true, for Mandelstam's "modernist" style goes back to his pre-Revolutionary verse; it is merely deepened in the poetry of the 1920s and 1930s.

5. Hartman, *The Unmediated Vision,* 173.

6. Dating the *Notebooks* varies somewhat. I follow the Baines–N. Mandelstam typescript in Baines, *Mandelstam,* 241–44. Shveitzer, *Voronezh Note-*

books, and Semenko. *Poetika pozdnego Mandel'shtama* agree with Baines. Levin, however, in "Zametki," 153–54, dates the *Third Moscow Notebook* from January 1937.

7. See Grigory Freidin's excellent analysis: "Mandel'shtam's Ode to Stalin: History and Myth," *Russian Review* 41, no. 4 (1982):400–26.

8. Nadezhda Mandelstam, *Hope Against Hope,* 83.

9. See *Osip Mandelstam: Selected Poems,* trans. Clarence Brown and W. S. Merwin (New York: Athenaeum, 1974), 69–70.

10. Freidin, "Mandel'shtam's Ode," finds interesting associations with Dante.

11. See "Return to Russia" in chapter 6.

12. See "Recovery of Poetic Obligation" in chapter 6.

13. See "'For some, winter is arrack'" in chapter 5.

14. Baines, *Mandelstam,* 112–20.

15. Mandelstam had seen the Vasilev brothers' film *Chapayev,* based on Furmanov's novel. Chapayev, the defiant hero throughout, would find a way to carry on *even after death.*

16. See Freidin, "Mandel'shtam's Ode."

17. Letter no. 85, *CPL,* 561.

18. Nadezhda Mandelstam, *Hope Against Hope,* chap. 43, "The Ode," 198–203.

19. Freidin, "Mandel'shtam's Ode," 421.

20. Freidin, in ibid., agrees that the "Ode" "seems to have been meant as an exorcism"; he also comments that it is "modelled on a magic spell" (419).

21. Several of Mandelstam's poems begin with similar lines or even stanzas, obviously stimulated by the same impulse that then led in different, even opposite, directions. These are known as "twin poems" rather than "variants" because, according to Nadezhda Mandelstam's comments in *Hope Against Hope* and *Hope Abandoned,* they were indeed separate.

22. Nadezhda Mandelstam, *Hope Against Hope,* 203.

23. See "Recovery of Poetic Obligation" in chapter 6.

24. See Levin, "Zametki o poezii O. Mandel'shtama tridtsatykh godov, II"; Omry Ronen, "K siuzhetu 'Stikhov o neizvestnom soldate' Mandel'shtama" (On the Plot of Mandelstam's "Verses on the Unknown Soldier"), *Slavica Hierosolymitana* 4 (1979):214–22; Semenko, *Poetika Pozdnego Mandel'shtama,* 102–26; Donald Rayfield, "Mandelstam's Voronezh Poetry," *Russian Literature Triquarterly* 11 (1975):323–62; Baines, *Mandelstam,* 208–16; Kiril Taranovsky, *Essays on Mandel'shtam,* 15–16. The text cited is based on *Voronezhskie tetradi,* ed. Victoria Shveitser with emendations by I. Semenko, *Poetika Pozdnego Mandel'shtama.* The English translation is based on D. Rayfield, with amendments and corrections based on Shveitzer, Baines, and Semenko.

25. See Baines, N. Mandelstam, and Semenko, *Poetika pozdnego Mandel'shtama.*

26. See "'For some, winter is arrack'" in chapter 5.

27. See the first half of chapter 5.

28. Lermontov was a stoop-shouldered poet.

29. Taranovsky, *Essays,* 15–16.

30. See "Words, Sounds, and Poetic Creation" in chapter 3.

31. Ronen, "K siuzhetu 'Stikhov o neizvestnom soldate' Mandel'-shtama," 218.

32. Ibid.

33. See chapter 3.

34. Natasha E. Shtempel, "Mandel'shtam v Voronezhe," *Novyi Mir* 10 (1987):207–236.

Selected Bibliography

PRIMARY SOURCES

Sobranie sochinenii (Collected works). 4 vols. Edited by Gleb Struve and Boris Filipoff. Vol. 1, Poetry, Washington, D.C.: Inter-Language Literary Associates, 1964; 2d ed., revised, 1967. Vol. 2, Poetry and Prose, Washington, D.C.: Inter-Language Literary Associates, 1966, 2d ed., revised 1971. Vol. 3, Essays and Letters, Washington, D.C.: Inter-Language Literary Associates, 1969. Vol. 4, Supplementary, Paris: YMCA Press, 1981. The most complete edition of Mandelstam's collected works in Russian; many detailed annotations.

Stikhotvoreniia (Poems). Edited by Nikolai I. Khardzhiev. Bol'shaia seriia (Poet's library, large series). Leningrad: Biblioteka poeta, 1974. The only post-Stalin edition of Mandelstam's verse. Khardzhiev's annotations are very useful, especially in conjunction with the notes available in the collected works.

Slovo i kul'tura: Stat'i (Word and Culture: Essays). Edited by Pavel Nerler. Introd. by M. Ia. Poliakov. Moscow: Sovetskii pisatel' (Soviet Writer), 1987. The first post-Stalin edition of Mandelstam's critical prose.

Voronezhskie Tetradi. (Voronezh Notebooks). Edited by Viktoria Shveitser. Ann Arbor, Mich.: Ardis, 1980. The *Voronezh Notebooks* according to Nadezhda Mandelstam's typescript.

The Complete Critical Prose and Letters. Edited by Jane G. Harris; translated by Jane G. Harris and Constance Link. Ann Arbor, Mich.: Ardis, 1979. The most complete collection in English of Mandelstam's prose and letters. Annotated translations of the poet's best-known and little-known literary essays, letters, literary and nonliterary prose (the excluded prose pieces, *Noise of Time* and *Egyptian Stamp,* are available in Brown).

The Noise of Time: The Prose of Osip Mandelstam. Translated by Clarence Brown. San Francisco: North Point Press, 1986. Translations of Mandelstam's best-known literary prose.

Selected Essays. Translated by Sidney Monas. Austin: University of Texas, 1977. Translations of selected literary essays.

Osip Mandelstam's "Stone." Translated by Robert Tracy. Princeton, N.J.: Princeton University Press, 1981. The translation of Mandelstam's first poetry collection.

Osip Mandelstam: Selected Poems. Translated by Clarence Brown and W. S. Merwin. New York: Athenaeum, 1974. Verse translations from various collections.

Osip Mandelstam: 50 Poems. Translated by Bernard Meares. New York: Persea Books, 1977. Verse translations from various collections.

Osip Mandelstam: Selected Poems. Translated David McDuff. Cambridge: Cambridge University Press, 1974. Verse translations from various collections.

Osip Mandelstam: Poems Chosen and Translated by James Greene. Boulder, Co.: Shambhala Publications, 1978. Verse translations from various collections.

SECONDARY SOURCES

Akhmatova, Anna. "Mandel'shtam (Listki iz dnevnika)" (Mandelstam: Pages from a diary). *Sobranie Sochinenii* (Collected Works). Edited by G. P. Struve and B. A. Filipoff. 2 vols. Washington, D.C.: Inter-language Literary Associates, 1968, 2:166–87. Translated by Kristin De Kuiper in *Russian Literature Triquarterly* 9 (1974):239–54. Brief but fascinating memoirs of Mandelstam by the poet closest to him.

Baines, Jennifer. *Mandelstam: The Later Poetry.* Cambridge: Cambridge University Press, 1976. A survey of the later poetry based on Nadezhda Mandelstam's manuscripts.

Brodsky, Joseph. "Preface." *Modern Russian Poets on Poetry.* Edited by Carl R. Proffer. Ann Arbor, Mich.: Ardis, 1974. An illuminating essay by a major contemporary Russian poet.

Brown, Clarence. *Mandelstam.* Cambridge: Cambridge University Press, 1973. The best biography of the poet. Also interesting analyses of his verse and essays up through 1925. Some biographical information on the later years.

Broyde, Steven. *Osip Mandelstam and His Age: Themes of War and Revolution.* Cambridge, Mass.: Harvard University Press, 1975. An excellent study of the poems treating war and revolution. Covers Mandelstam's verse and essays through the 1920s.

Eikhenbaum, Boris. "O Mandel'shtame (14 Marta 1933)" (On Mandelstam [14 March 1933])" *Den' poezii* (Poetry day) 1967: 167–68. The only available source on Mandelstam's last reading in Leningrad, March 1933.

Erenburg, Il'ia G. (chair). "Vecher pamiati Mandel'shtama v MGU, 13 maia, 1965 g. Mekhmat. Predsedatel' Erenburg" (Memorial evening for Mandelstam on 1 May 1965 at Moscow State University). *Grani* (Facets) 77 (1970): 82–88. An account of the first public efforts to rehabilitate

Mandelstam—a reading of his verse at Moscow University, May 1965.

Freidin, Grigory. *A Coat of Many Colors.* Berkeley: University of California Press, 1987. Unavailable when this book went to press.

————. "Mandel'shtam's *Ode to Stalin*: History and Myth." *Russian Review* 41 no. 4 (1982):400–26. An excellent analysis of the "Stalin Ode."

Gershtein, Emma G. *Novoe o Mandel'shtame* (New Materials on Mandelstam) Paris: Atheneum, 1986. Interesting memoir materials about the 1930s.

Gifford, Henry. "Mandelstam and the *Journey*." In *Mandelstam: Journey to Armenia.* San Francisco: George F. Ritchie, 1979. Valuable essay on *Journey to Armenia.*

Ginzburg, Lidiia. "Poetika Osipa Mandel'shtama" (The poetics of Osip Mandelstam)/ *O starom i novom* (On the olde and new). Leningrad: Sovetskii pisatel' (Soviet writer), 1982. In English, see "The Poetics of Osip Mandelstam." Translated by Sona Hoisington in *Twentieth Century Russian Literary Criticism.* Edited by Victor Ehrlich. New Haven, Conn.: Yale University Press, 1974. (Based on a 1972 version of the above.) A brief but exceedingly insightful interpretation of Mandelstam's oeuvre.

Gumilev, Nikolai. Review of Mandel'shtam's *Kamen'* (Stone) in *Apollon* 1–2 (1914) and 1 (1916). In *Sobranie sochinenii.* Edited by G. P. Struve and B. A. Filipoff. 4 vols. Washington, D. C.: Inter-Language Literary Associates, 1962–68. The earliest published critiques of Mandelstam's verse.

Harris, Jane G. "Autobiographical Theory and the Problem of Esthetic Coherence in Mandelstam's *Noise of Time*." *Essays in Poetics* 9, no. 2 (1984):33–66. Mandelstam's autobiographical prose in the context of theories of autobiography.

————. "The Latin Gerundive as Autobiographical Imperative: Reading Mandelstam's *Journey to Armenia*." *Slavic Review* 45, no. 1 (1986):1–19. A study of the *Journey to Armenia.*

Isenberg, Charles. "Associative chains in 'Egipetskaia marka.'" *Russian Literature* 5, no. 3 (1977): 257–76. A most valuable interpretation of *Egyptian Stamp.*

Koubourlis, Demetrius J., Editor. *A Concordance to the Poems of Osip Mandelstam.* Ithaca, N.Y.: Cornell University Press, 1974. A concordance to the poetry.

Kuzin, Boris S. "Ob O. E. Mandel'shtame" (On Mandelstam). *Vestnik Russkogo Khristianskogo Dvizheniia (VRKhD)* (Herald of the Rusian Christian Movement [Paris]), 140 (1983):99–129. (Memoirs are dated October 1970.) Some interesting memoir materials about Mandelstam in Armenia.

Levin, Iurii I. "O nekotorykh chertakh plana soderzhaniia v poeticheskom tekste" (On Certain elements of the plane of content in a poetic text). *Strukturnaia tipologiia* (Structural Typology), 1966, 199–215. The best

Soviet interpreter of Mandelstam's verse.

————. "O nekotorykh chertakh plana soderzhaniia v poeticheskikh tekstakh. Materialy k izucheniiu poetiki O. Mandel'shtama" (On certain elements of the plane of content in Poetic texts. Materials for the study of Mandelstam's poetics). *International Journal of Slavic Linguistics and Poetics* (*IJSLP*) 12 1969): 106–64.

————. "Zametki k 'Razgovoru o Dante' O. Mandel'shtama" (Notes on Mandelstam's *Conversation about Dante*). *International Journal of Slavic Lingusitics and Poetics* 15 (1972):184–97.

————. "Razbor dvukh stikhotvorenii Mandel'shtama" (An analysis of two poems of Mandelstam's). *Russian Literature* 2 (1973): 37–49.

————. "Razbor odnogo stikhotvoreniia Mandel'shtama" (An analysis of one of Mandelstam's poems). *Slavic Poetics. Essays in Honor of Kiril Taranovsky*. The Hague: Mouton, 1973.

————. "O chastotnom slovare iazyka poeta: imena sushchestvitel'nye u Osipa Mandel'shtama" (On a Frequency dictionary of the poet's language: Nouns in Mandelstam). *Russian Literature* 2 (1973): 5–36.

————. "O sootnoshenii mezhdu semantikoi poeticheskogo teksta i vnetekstovoi real'nostiu" (On the Relationship between the semantics of a poetic text and external reality). *Russian Literature* 10, no. 11 (1975): 147–72.

————. "Zametki o 'Krymsko-ellinskikh stikhakh O Mandel'shtama" (Notes on Mandelstam's "Crimean-Hellenic poems"). *Russian Literature* 10, no. 11 (1975): 5–31.

————. "Razbor odnogo stikhotvoreniia Osipa Mandel'shtama" (An analysis of one of Osip Mandelstam's poems). *Russian Literature* 5, no. 2 (1977): 115–22.

————. "Zametki o poezii Osipa Mandel'shtama 30-x godov, I" (Notes on Mandelstam's poetry of the 1930s). *Slavica Hierosolymitana* 3 (1978): 110–73.

————. "Zametki o poezii Osipa Mandel'shtama tridtsatykh godov, II ('Stikhi o neizvestnom soldate')" (Notes on Mandelstam's poetry of the 1930s ["Verses on the Unknown Soldier"]). *Slavica Hierosolymitana* 4 (1979): 185–213.

————. "Semanticheskii analiz stikhotvoreniia. Teoriia poeticheskoi rechi i poeticheskaia leksikografiia" (Semantic analysis of poetry. Theory of poetic speech and poetic lexicography). *Teoriia Poeticheskoi Rechi i Poeticheskaia Leksikografiia* (Theory of poetic speech and poetic lexicography). Shadrinsk, 1971.

————. "Masteritsa vinovatykh vzorov' O. Mandel'shtama" (Mandelstam's "Master of Guilty Glances" [revision of 1971 article with commentary by Mikhail Lotman]). *Uchebnyi Material po Analizu Poeticheskikh Tekstov* (Study materials for the analysis of poetic texts). Tallin, 1982.

Levin, Iurii; Segal, Dmitrii; Timenchik, Roman D.; Toporov, V.; Tsivian, T. "Russkaia semanticheskaia poetika kak potensial'naia kul'turnaia paradigma" (Russian semantic poetics as a potential cultural paradigm). *Russian Literature* 7, no. 8 (1974): 47–82.

Levinton, G. A. "Na kamennykh otrogakh Pierii Mandel'shtama: materialy k analizu" (Mandelstam's "On the Rocky Spurs of Pieria": materials for analysis). *Russian Literature* 5, no. 2 (1977):123–70; 3 (1977):201–36. Excellent study of the Crimean poems.

Mandelstam, Nadezhda. *Hope Against Hope.* Translated by Max Hayward. New York: Athenaeum, 1972. (*Vospominaniia.* New York: Chekhov Publishing House, 1970) The first volume of Nadezhda Mandelstam's memoirs. Extremely valuable portrait of life under Stalinism.

————. *Hope Abandoned.* Translated by Max Hayward. New York: Athenaeum, 1974. (*Vtoraia kniga.* Paris: YMCA Press, 1972.) Second volume of memoirs by N. Mandelstam. Just as valuable as the first volume but more vituperative.

Mints, Zinaida G. "Voennye Astry" (Military asters). *Vtorichnye Modeliruiushchie Sistemy* (Secondary modeling systems). Tartu: Tartuskii Gos. Universitet, 1979. A valuable study of the poem, "Voennye astry. . . ."

Morozov, A. A. Introduction to *Mandel'shtam. Razgovor o Dante.* Moscow, 1967. Introduction to the first Soviet publication of *Conversation about Dante.*

————. "Mandel'shtam v zapiskakh dnevnika S.P. Kablukova" (Mandelstam in the diary entries of S. P. Kablukov). *Vestnik Russkogo Khristianskogo Dvizheniia* (Herald of the Rusian Christian Movement [Paris]) 129, no. 3 (1979):134–55. Valuable memoir materials.

Mureddu, Donata. "Mandelstam and Petrarch." *Scando-Slavica* (Copenhagen) 26 (1979): 53–84. A fine essay on Mandelstam's Petrarchan sonnets.

Nerler, P. "K 90–letiiu so dnia rozhdeniia O.E. Mandel'shtama" (On the ninetieth anniversary of Mandelstam's birth). *Literaturnaia Gazeta* (Literary Gazette)3 (14 January 1981), 6. Notes by the present head of the Mandelstam Commission celebrating the ninetieth anniversary of the poet's birth.

Nilsson, Nils A. *Osip Mandelstam: Five Poems.* Vol. 1. Stockholm: Stockhom Studies in Russian Literature, 1974. Excellent readings of five major poems.

Pamiat'. Istoricheskii sbornik vospominanii, ocherkov (Memory. Historical almanac of memoirs and sketches). Vol. 2 Moscow-Paris: YMCA Press, 1977/ 1979; vol. 4 1979/81. Some interesting memoirs.

Przybylski, Riszard. *Wdzieczny Gosc Boga* (God's Greatful Guest). Paris: Libella, 1980. An interesting scholarly study of Mandelstam's early verse in Polish. An English translation is available from Ardis Publishers.

Rayfield, Donald. "Mandelstam's Voronezh Poetry." *Russian Literature Triquarterly* 11 (1975): 323–62. A useful study of some of the later poetry.

Ronen, Omry. "Mandelstam's Kashchej.'" *Studies for Professor Roman Jakobson.* Cambridge, Mass: Harvard University Press, 1968.

————. "Leksicheskij povtor, podtekst i smysl v poetike Osipa Mandel'-

shtama" (Lexical repetition, subtext and meaning in Mandelstam's poetics). *Slavic Poetics*. The Hague: Mouton, 1973.

―――. "The Dry River and the Black Ice: anamnesis and amnesia in Mandelstam's poem 'Ja slovo pozabyl, chto ja khotel skazat.'" *Slavica Hierosolymitana* 1 (1977): 177–84.

―――. "A Beam upon the Axe: some antecedents of Osip Mandelstam's 'Umyvalsja noch'ju na dvore.'" *Slavica Hierosolymitana* 1 (1977): 158–76.

―――. "K siuzhetu 'Stikhov o neizvestnom soldate' Mandel'shtama" (On the plot of Mandelstam's "Verses on the Unknown Soldier"). *Slavica Hierosolymitana* 4 (1979):214—22.

―――. *An Approach to Mandel'stam. Jerusalem*: The Magnes Press, 1983. An invaluable study of the longer narrative poems "Slate Ode" and "January 1, 1924" by a major Mandelstam scholar.

Segal, Dmitry M. "Nabliudeniia nad semanticheskoi struktury poeticheskogo proizvedeniia" (Observations on the semantic structure of a poetic work). *International Journal of Slavic Linguistics and Poetics* 11 (1968): 159–71. A major Mandelstam scholar.

―――. "O nekotorykh aspektakh semanticheskoi struktury 'Grifel'noi ody'" (On certain aspects of the semantic structure of "Slate Ode"). *Russian Literature* 2 (1972): 49–102.

―――. "Mikrosemantika odnogo stikhotvoreniia Mandel'shtama" (Microsemantics of one of Mandelstam's poems). *Slavic Poetics* (1973).

―――. "Voprosy poeticheskoi organizatsii semantiki v proze Mandel'shtama" (Problems of poetic organization of semantics in Mandelstam's prose). *Russian Poetics: Proceedings of the International Colloquium at the University of California at Los Angeles, September 22–26, 1975*. Edited by Thomas Eekman and Dean S. Worth, UCLA Slavic Series, vol. 4 (Los Angeles: University of California, 1983).

―――. "Fragment semanticheskoi poetiki O. E. Mandel'shtama" (A fragment of the semantic poetics of Mandelstam). *Russian Literature* 10, no. 11 (1975): 59–147.

―――. "Eshche odin neizvestnyi tekst Mandel'shtama" (Another undiscovered text of Mandelstam). *Slavica Hierosolymitana* 3 (1978):174–92.

―――. "Literatura kak okhranaia gramota" (Literature as letter of safe conduct). *Slavica Hierosolymitana* 5–6 (1981): 151–244.

Semenko, Irina M. "Osip Mandel'shtam. Zapisnye knizhki. Zametki" (Osip Mandelstam. Notebooks. Notes). *Voprosy literatury* (Problems of literature) 4 (1968):180–204. A textological study of Mandelstam's notebooks for *Journey to Armenia*.

―――. *Poetika Pozdnego Mandel'shtama* (Poetics of the late Mandelstam). Rome: Carruci editore, 1986. A collection of textological analyses of several of Mandelstam's most complex poems of the 1920s and 1930s.

Steiner, Peter. "Poem as Manifesto: Mandel'stam's 'Notre Dame.'" *Russian Literature* 5, no. 3 (1977):239–56. An excellent analysis of "Notre Dame," Mandelstam's Acmeist manifesto in verse.

Shtempel, Natasha E. "Mandel'shtam v Voronezhe," *Novyi Mir* 10 (1987):207–236. Interesting memoirs about Mandelstam's last years, 1936–1937.

Struve, Nikita. *Ossip Mandelstam.* Paris: YMCA Press, 1982. An interesting religio-biographical study of Mandelstam's work.

Tager, Elena M. "O Mandel'shtame. Vospominaniia" (Memoirs. About Mandelstam). *Novyi zhurnal* (New Review) 81 (1965):172–99. Interesting memoir materials.

Taranovksy, Kiril F. *Essays on Mandel'stam.* Cambridge, Mass.: Harvard University Press, 1976. A collection of the outstanding essays of this well-known Mandelstam scholar.

Terras, Victor. "Classical Motifs in the Poetry of Mandel'stam." *Slavic and East European Journal* 10, no. 3 (1966): 251–67. Interesting analyses of Mandelstam's philosophical and classical motifs.

———. "The Time Philosophy of Osip Mandel'stam." *Slavonic and East European Review* 47 (1969):344–54.

———. "Osip Mandel'stam i ego filosofiia slova." *Slavic Poetics* (1973):455–60.

Toddes, E. A. "Mandelstam i Tiutchev." *International Journal of Slavic Linguistics and Poetics* 17 (1974):59–85. On Mandelstam's early verse and its Tiutchevian subtexts.

———. "Mandel'shtam i opoiazovskaia filologiia" (Mandelstam and the philology of *Opoyaz*). *Tynianovskii Sbornik: Vtorye Tynianovskie Chteniia* (Tynianov miscellany: second volume of Readings [Riga: "Zinatne"]) (1986):78–102. On Mandelstam and the formalists.

Tsvetaeva, Marina. "Istoriia odnogo posviashcheniia" (History of a dedication). *Oxford Slavonic Papers* 11 (1964): 112–36. Amusing memoir of Tsvetaeva's meeting with Mandelstam in 1916.

Tynianov, Iurii. "Promezhutok" (Interlude). *Arkhaisty i novatory* (Archaists and Innovators). Leningrad (1925). An excellent early analysis of Mandelstam's verse.

West, Daphne. *Mandelstam: The Egyptian Stamp.* Birmingham Slavonic Monographs 10, Birmingham 1980. A study of Mandelstam's novella.

Zhirmunskii, Viktor. "Preodolevshie simvolizm" (Those who superseded symbolism). *Russkaia mysl'* (Russian thought) 12, reprint (1916); *Voprosy teorii literatury: Stat'i* (Problems of literary theory: articles) 1916–1926. Leningrad: Academia, 1928, 302–13. One of the first analyses of *Stone*.

Zholkovsky, Alexander K. "Invarianty i struktura teksta.II. Osip Mandel'shtam: 'Ia p'iu za voennye astry'" (Invariants and structure of the text:II. Osip Mandelstam's "I Drink to Military Asters"). *Slavica Hierosolymitana* 4 (1979): 159–84. Fine analysis of poem "Voennye astry."

Index